WATCH IT, SAILOR!

A Comedy in Three Acts

by

PHILIP KING

and

FALKLAND L. CARY

SAMUEL   FRENCH

LONDON

NEW YORK   TORONTO   SYDNEY   HOLLYWOOD

© 1961 BY PHILIP KING AND FALKLAND L. CARY

SAMUEL FRENCH LTD, 26 SOUTHAMPTON STREET, STRAND, LONDON WC2, or their authorized agents, issue licences to amateurs to give performances of this play on payment of a fee. **The fee must be paid, and the licence obtained, before a performance is given.**

Licences are issued subject to the understanding that it shall be made clear in all advertising matter that the audience will witness an amateur performance; and that the names of the authors of plays shall be included on all announcements and on all programmes.

The royalty fee indicated below is subject to contract and subject to variation at the sole discretion of Samuel French Ltd.

Fee for one performance
of this play by amateurs   £5.25
in the British Isles

Fee for each subsequent
consecutive performance   £4.20
at the same theatre or hall

In territories overseas the fee quoted above may not apply. Application must be made to our local authorized agents, or if there is no such agent, to Samuel French Ltd, London.

Applications to perform the play by professionals should be made to ERIC GLASS LTD, 28 Berkeley Square, London, W1.

ISBN 0 573 01472 8

MADE AND PRINTED IN GREAT BRITAIN BY
LATIMER TREND AND CO LTD PLYMOUTH
MADE IN ENGLAND

WATCH IT, SAILOR!

Produced by Toby Rowland Ltd, in association with Pertpic Ltd and Cedric B. Levitt at the Aldwych Theatre, London, on the 24th February, 1960, with the following cast of characters:

(in the order of their appearance)

SHIRLEY HORNETT	*Josephine Massey*
ALBERT TUFNELL, A.B.	*Ian Curry*
DAPHNE PINK	*Wanda Ventham*
CARNOUSTIE BLIGH, A.B.	*Fraser Kerr*
HENRY HORNETT	*Cyril Smith*
EDIE HORNETT	*Esma Cannon*
EMMA HORNETT	*Kathleen Harrison*
MRS LACK	*Ann Lancaster*
LIEUT-COMMANDER HARDCASTLE, R.N.	*Stanley Beard*

Directed by HENRY KENDALL and ANDRE VAN GYSEGHEM

Setting by KEN CALDER

SYNOPSIS OF SCENES

The action of the Play passes in the living-room of the Hornetts' home

ACT I
Late morning

ACT II
Five minutes later

ACT III
Immediately following

ACT I

SCENE—*The living-room of the Hornetts' home. Late morning.*
There is a door up R leading to the kitchen and thence to the back entrance.
A door L leads to the hall, front door and staircase. The fireplace is down R.
A casement window back C overlooks the garden. There is a cupboard up L,
under the projection of the staircase. The furnishings are ordinary in taste;
everything about the room is spotless. There is a sofa LC and a small dining-
table stands RC with upright chairs R and above it. Below the fireplace,
down R, there are shelves in front of which is a pouffe. An easy chair stands
by the fireside. Above the fireplace there is a small table with a radio and
a small sideboard. Upright chairs stand L of the window and below the door
L. Down L there is a trolley and R of the window there is a tall stand with a
potted plant on it. The Hornetts are a working-class family.

When the CURTAIN rises, the room is empty. The right half of the window is
open. HENRY's jacket, tie and stiff collar are on the back of the easy chair.
On the table are SHIRLEY's bridal veil and bouquet and DAPHNE's posy.
SHIRLEY HORNETT runs on L, followed by ALBERT TUFNELL, A.B.
SHIRLEY is pretty and aged twenty. She is in her wedding dress. ALBERT
is twenty-three, good-looking and brimming over with good health and good
spirits. He is self-possessed but not aggressively so. In short, ALBERT is the
ideal sailor girls dream about. He wears A.B. uniform with the regulation
white wedding ribbon. SHIRLEY laughingly evades ALBERT, who chases
her around the room.

SHIRLEY (*running to R of the table*) No, Albert, no! Not before the wedding!

ALBERT (L *of the table*) Damn the wedding!

SHIRLEY. Albert Tufnell!

ALBERT (*moving above the table towards Shirley*) No! I didn't mean that, Shirl . . .

SHIRLEY (*dodging below the table and then above the sofa*) I should hope not, indeed!

ALBERT (*laughingly*) What I meant was I want a kiss *now*, and I'm having one—wedding or no wedding. (*He advances on her*)

SHIRLEY (*dodging L of the sofa, then below it to C*) But—it's—it's supposed to be unlucky, isn't it, for the bridegroom to kiss the bride before they go to church?

ALBERT (*smiling*) Even when it's for the second time in one morning? (*He moves quietly to L of her*)

SHIRLEY (*falteringly*) I—I don't know. I'm the first bride I know who's had to do that—thanks to you. (*With a half smile*) I shall never forgive you, Albert, for what you did. Never.

ALBERT (*taking her hands in his*) You'll forgive, all right. But you'll

never *forget* why I did it, Shirl. And—(*with a laugh*) in years to come
—when our own son is getting married . . .

SHIRLEY (*snuggling up to him*) Albert!

ALBERT. That's right. He'll be called "Albert".

SHIRLEY. Silly! You know I didn't mean that.

ALBERT (*smoothly*) And if he's marrying a girl with a dragon of
a mother . . .

SHIRLEY. Albert!

ALBERT. Sorry! Let's say with a mother like yours—it comes to
the same thing, anyway. (*Before Shirley can protest again*) *If* he's marrying a girl with a mother like that, I hope you'll tell him why his own
father didn't turn up at the church the first time. Because he wanted
to show you that once you were married you'd got to be *his* wife and
to cut loose from your mother's apron strings. You'll tell Albert
Tufnell Junior—that—won't you, Shirl?

SHIRLEY. Oh, my darling!

(*They go into a big embrace*)

(*She pushes him away, crosses to the fireplace and looks in the mirror over
the mantelpiece*) Albert, I'm going to be firm.

ALBERT. I hope you *are*. You'll need to be. That mother of yours!

SHIRLEY. I mean with *you*, Albert Tufnell. There'll be no more
nonsense until after the wedding. (*She turns, realizing what she has said*)
I—I mean—well, you know what I mean.

ALBERT (*crossing to her; with a smile*) I have an idea. (*He embraces
her*)

(DAPHNE PINK *and* CARNOUSTIE BLIGH, A.B. *enter* L. DAPHNE *is
a smart, streamlined and salesman-like piece of goods, with a charming
manner and an attractive smile. She wears a bridesmaid's dress.* CAR-
NOUSTIE *is about the same age as Albert and has his manly beauty, but it
inclines to be severe. He takes life seriously, but is extremely popular with
his mates, and, to his embarrassment, women are apt to fall for him. His
Scottish nationality is not for one moment in doubt once he opens his mouth.
He wears sailor's uniform with the regulation white wedding ribbon*)

DAPHNE (*smiling*) I hope we're not interrupting?

SHIRLEY (*breaking from Albert*) No, no. We were just—just . . .

DAPHNE (*smiling*) I know you were—we could see that for our-
selves. Couldn't we, Carnoustie?

CARNOUSTIE (*embarrassed*) Daphne!

DAPHNE. Albert, I wish you'd give this best man of yours a few
lessons.

ALBERT. What on, Daphne?

DAPHNE. How to make love. You hold a woman as if she's—a
woman.

CARNOUSTIE. Hold your whist!

DAPHNE. Scottie, here, holds me as if I was a set of bagpipes.

CARNOUSTIE. Ye're awful!

ALBERT (*with a wink*) Funny you should say that about him, Daphne.

DAPHNE. Funny? Why?

ALBERT. It was Carnoustie, here, who taught me all I know.

CARNOUSTIE (*shocked*) Albert! How can you say such a thing. (*To Daphne*) Daphne, don't listen to him.

SHIRLEY (*moving below the table*) Stop talking nonsense, both of you. Albert, it will soon be time for you and Carnoustie to be getting down to the church again.

DAPHNE. Yes. But, Shirley, you're not going to the church like that, I hope.

SHIRLEY. Like what?

DAPHNE. I can understand how it's happened, of course, but I doubt if your mother would.

SHIRLEY. What are you talking about?

DAPHNE. Your lipstick. (*She indicates Shirley's lips by putting her finger on her own lips*)

SHIRLEY. Oh! (*She rushes to the mirror R and is horrified at what she sees*) Oh, my goodness! (*To Albert. With mock anger*) And it took me twenty minutes to get that right.

ALBERT. Shirl . . .

(SHIRLEY *crosses and dashes off* L. ALBERT *follows her across and stands above the sofa*)

DAPHNE (*to Albert*) And you look as if you've been buzzing round the jam-pot.

CARNOUSTIE (*muttering*) I dinna like all this nonsense. (*He sits C of the sofa*)

(ALBERT *takes out his handkerchief, wipes his mouth, then sits R of Carnoustie on the sofa*)

DAPHNE (*crossing to R of the sofa*) Albert, I'm not being suspicious, but you are getting married this time, aren't you? Or—*don't* tell me you've changed your mind *again*? Not *twice* in one morning.

ALBERT. Of course I haven't. I'm going through with it this time.

DAPHNE (*moving below the sofa*) So I should hope. (*To Carnoustie*) Move over.

(CARNOUSTIE *moves along the sofa seat to the left end of it*)

(*She sits between Albert and Carnoustie on the sofa*) Albert, I shall never forget this morning as long as I live. If you could've *seen* us all at the church—waiting for you to turn up.

CARNOUSTIE. It was awfu'. A've never felt so ashamed in ma life.

DAPHNE. And, Albert, if you could have seen Aunt Emma's face.

CARNOUSTIE. Aye! She looked like Frankenstein. An' puir wee Shirley. Ma heart bled for her. It bled for you, too, Daphne.

DAPHNE. Then you lost a lot of blood for nothing, 'cos I had the giggles.

CARNOUSTIE (*in horror*) What?

DAPHNE. Well, all I could think of was—(*she sings quietly*) "There was I, waiting at the church, waiting at the church . . ."

ALBERT (*rising and crossing to the fireplace*) Turn it up, Daphne.

DAPHNE. I'm sorry, Albert, but truth will out. Look, I'm very fond of Shirley, even if she is my cousin, but I think you did the right thing by not turning up this morning.

CARNOUSTIE. You do?

DAPHNE (*turning to Carnoustie; firmly*) I do. (*She suddenly points a finger accusingly at Carnoustie*) But don't you try that on at *our* wedding, my lad.

CARNOUSTIE (*fervently*) A' won't! (*He rises indignantly*) Here! What d'y' mean—"our wedding"? A' havena' proposed to you.

DAPHNE (*practically and almost casually*) I know you haven't, but you're going to.

CARNOUSTIE (*gaping*) What?

DAPHNE. We'll get *Albert* settled first.

CARNOUSTIE (*babbling*) But a've only known you a night and a day.

DAPHNE. What's that got to do with it? You sit down and be quiet. (*She pulls Carnoustie down on to the sofa*) Albert, you showed Aunt Emma that you weren't going to let her rule your life. You stood up to her and you won.

ALBERT. I wonder.

(*Women's voices are heard off outside the window.* ALBERT *crosses to the window and glances out*)

DAPHNE. Of course you did. She's a changed woman, thanks to you. And now you and Shirley *are* getting married after all, and you're beginning as you mean to go on, and I'm proud of you.

ALBERT. Bless you, Daphne.

DAPHNE. Granted you're getting married at one o'clock instead of *eleven*, but you'll still be on your honeymoon in Brighton *tonight*, and—(*with a very knowing smile*) it's *that* that counts—(*she turns to Carnoustie, winks and digs him in the ribs*) eh, Scottie?

CARNOUSTIE (*firmly*) Don't involve me in your doubtful innuendoes.

DAPHNE (*to Albert*) Isn't he sweet? And I love him.

(ALBERT *closes the window and shuts out the sound of the voices*)

ALBERT. You know, that little lot's not going to help much.

CARNOUSTIE. What lot?

ALBERT (*moving above the sofa*) All those women waiting to see what happens next. We've got to go through that mob again.

CARNOUSTIE (*mournfully*) Aye! This hoose *would* be the last but one in the street. A'll never reach the main road. I'll die of mortification.

DAPHNE (*scornfully*) Now you're never scared of facing a pack of silly women, are you?

CARNOUSTIE (*mournfully*) I'd sooner stand on the burning deck when all but me had fled.

(*The kitchen door opens cautiously.*

HENRY HORNETT *peeps in from the kitchen. He is a smallish man of fifty. He is in his shirt-sleeves*)

HENRY (*looking around*) Hullo!

ALBERT. Hullo, Pop. What are you doing—peeping in?

HENRY. Just peeping in. (*With caution*) Where's Emma?

ALBERT. She's not here. (*He perches on the back of the sofa*)

HENRY (*coming into the room*) Thank the Lord! (*He shivers*)

DAPHNE. What's the matter, Uncle Henry, you're not cold, are you?

HENRY. 'Course I'm not.

DAPHNE. But you shivered.

HENRY. It's the quiet, the quiet of this house.

DAPHNE. Yes, it is quiet—come to think of it.

HENRY. It always is—before the storm bursts. (*He takes his collar and tie from the easy chair, looks in the mirror and slowly puts them on*)

(DAPHNE *rises*)

ALBERT ⎫
DAPHNE ⎬ (*together*) ⎰ (*He rises; alarmed*) What do you mean, Pop? You don't mean that Mrs Hornett . . . ?
⎱ Storm? Uncle, nothing's gone wrong, has it?

HENRY (*dubiously*) No, nothing's gone wrong. (*He turns*)

CARNOUSTIE (*with relief*) Oh! My heart was in my mouth for a moment. I thought . . .

ALBERT. Sit down, Carnoustie.

CARNOUSTIE. Eh?

ALBERT. Sit down.

(CARNOUSTIE *resumes his seat, apprehension showing on his face*)

(*Quietly but firmly*) Now, come on, Pop—what's worrying you? You said nothing's gone wrong. Well . . .

HENRY. Nor it 'as—yet.

(EDIE HORNETT *enters quietly from the kitchen. She is a thin, nondescript spinster of fortyish. She is vaguely wiping a saucer and listens apprehensively to Henry*)

But it just wants one little thing to upset Emma—one little spark, and it'll be Guy Fawkes Night all over again.

EDIE (*moving to L of Henry; in agony*) Oh, don't, Henry! I couldn't stand it—not again. Not after what we went through this morning.

(ALBERT *resignedly perches on the right arm of the sofa*)

HENRY (*desperately*) Now look, Edie, why don't you keep out of this?

DAPHNE (*to Henry; desperately*) Uncle, never mind Aunt Edie. You don't really think . . . ?

HENRY (*to Daphne*) If we can only get Albert, here, and Shirley to the church before Emma explodes again—and she's going to explode again, you can take my word for that. But so long as it 'appens after the wedding and not before, I'll be so grateful I'll join the Salvation Army.

EDIE. Do you think if I took her a cup of tea . . . ?

HENRY. Yes, if you could slip a Bob Martin's into it.

EDIE (*whimpering*) If only things had gone right this morning. (*To Albert*) If only you hadn't left Shirley at the altar rails—(*whimpering more*) just like I was left with my Great Sorrow . . .

HENRY. For the Lord's sake don't start bringing that up, you and your ruddy Great Sorrow.

EDIE (*wildly*) But don't you see, Henry. What happened to Shirley's like what happened to me.

HENRY. It's not what happened to you at all. You were left at the altar rails twenty years ago and as far as the chap you were going to marry's concerned, you're *still* waiting.

(EDIE *howls*)

Now, Albert, here, 'e didn't turn up, but he was man enough to come back and tell us why he didn't, and he even had the guts to tell Emma just where she got off, and now everything's supposed to be Hunky-Dory between the two of them and the wedding's on again in half an hour. Have you got that clear?

EDIE. I think so, Henry. Yes, I think so. You think Emma's going to explode again, and if that doesn't happen until after the wedding, you're going to join the Salvation Army. (*She sings and uses the saucer as a tambourine*) "At the end of the journey we shall wear a crown . . ." I hope you do join, Henry. It'll get you out in the fresh air. And the uniform'll suit you, Henry. Pity it's blue. It *does* show the dust so much. (*She dissolves into tears*)

ALBERT. Blimey!

DAPHNE (*moving to Edie and putting an arm around her*) Now, come on, Aunt Edie. You come and sit down. Pull yourself together. (*She sits Edie in the chair above the table and stands behind her*)

EDIE. Yes, I must. I must. If Emma sees me—it might just be that spark Henry mentioned—the one to cause the explosion. (*She whimpers*) And I can't stand bangs.

ALBERT (*rising and moving to L of the table*) But, Pop, nothing's upset Mrs Hornett *so far*—has it?

HENRY. That's nothing to sing hymns about.

ALBERT. Oh, hell! You've got me quaking, Pop. What can we do to keep her happy?

HENRY (*morosely*) All *you* might do is—break your neck.

EDIE   } (*together*) { Oh, what a terrible thing to say.
ALBERT }   { What?

(EDIE *rises, moves to the window and looks out*)

HENRY. And if that doesn't appeal to you, then all you can do is watch, pray and—say nothing.

CARNOUSTIE (*plaintively*) But, Mr Hornett, Albert and your daughter are getting married. And a wedding's supposed to be a joyous occasion.

HENRY. I know it is. But I hope neither you nor Albert will be such damn fools as to show any jollity for the next twenty minutes or so.

ALBERT (*crossing to L of the sofa*) But, Pop . . .

HENRY (*breaking in quickly*) I grant you it's bad luck on *you*, Albert; not being able to show jollity *before* your wedding—'cos believe me, you'll show ruddy little after.

(EDIE *suddenly gives a scream of horror and opens the window. The women's voices are heard. The others are startled*)

What the 'ell . . . ?

EDIE (*wildly*) That cat!

HENRY (*rushing to R of Edie; alarmed*) What?

(DAPHNE *moves behind Henry.* ALBERT *moves to L of Edie. They all look out of the window*)

EDIE. Mrs Mottram's cat—it's in our garden again. If Emma sees it . . . (*With another big yell*) Oh, Henry! Look what it's about to commence to do. (*She calls wildly*) Pussy, stop it! You mustn't!

HENRY (*grabbing an ornament from the window-sill; shouting*) Out of the way, Edie. (*He raises the ornament as if to fling it*)

EDIE (*grabbing Henry's arm; wilder still*) No, Henry! *No!* You mustn't throw that—it's Emma's favourite little piece. (*She takes the ornament from Henry*)

HENRY (*fuming*) I'll murder that cat.

EDIE. It's all right, Henry. It's finished. Oh, thank heaven Emma didn't see it. (*She puts the ornament on the window-sill and turns*) Would you like a cup of tea?

(ALBERT *and* CARNOUSTIE *solemnly shake their heads.* ALBERT *closes the window and the voices fade*)

Tea, Daphne?

(DAPHNE *shakes her head*)

Henry? Tea? (*Before Henry has time to reply, her eyes light on the bouquet and posy on the table. She picks them up and peers at them*) Oh. Shirley's bouquet and your posy, Daphne. I wonder if they ought to have a drink?

HENRY (*crossing to the fireplace*) Yes, and a cup of tea each ought to finish 'em off nicely.

EDIE. I wasn't thinking of tea, Henry, I . . .

(DAPHNE *joins Albert at the window*)

HENRY (*plaintively*) Now look, Edie, why don't you disappear for a bit?

EDIE. What?

HENRY. You're not coming to the wedding *this* time, either—are you?

EDIE (*moving to* L *of Henry; whimpering*) No, 'Enry, I couldn't bring myself to.

HENRY (*heartily*) Good!

EDIE. I'd love to. I'd love to, but . . .

ALBERT. Then why don't you, Aunt Edie? (*He moves and sits* R *of Carnoustie on the sofa*)

HENRY. Don't you worry, Albert, you'll have enough to cope with without her and her Great Sorrow thrown in. (*To Edie*) Why don't you go somewhere and be 'appy for a change—just for a few hours?

EDIE (*whimpering*) But where can I go?

HENRY. Anywhere. Abyssinia—Afghanistan . . .

EDIE (*dissolving into tears*) No, I'll go into the kitchen.

(*A door is heard to slam upstairs.* EDIE *gives a terrified gulp.* ALBERT *and* CARNOUSTIE *sit up rigid.* DAPHNE *sits on the chair* L *of the window.* HENRY *stands rigid.* DAPHNE *sits on the chair* L *of the window.* HENRY *stands rigid at the fireplace*)

HENRY ⎫
EDIE ⎭ (*together; as if announcing the end of the world*) Emma!

HENRY (*to Edie; jerking his thumb towards the kitchen*) Beat it! Or look as if you're doing something.

EDIE (*moving to the kitchen door; breathlessly*) I'll beat it.

(EDIE *exits to the kitchen, taking the bouquet and posy with her.* HENRY *picks up his jacket from the easy chair, puts it on, then stands with his back to the room, watching in the mirror.*

EMMA HORNETT *enters* L *at great speed. She is a woman of Edie's age, masterful and sharp-tongued. One knows immediately that she is spoiling for "battle". It is only with a superhuman effort that she holds herself in check.* ALBERT, CARNOUSTIE *and* DAPHNE *watch Emma, almost transfixed.* EMMA *looks at them for a moment, then turns away, very quickly removes her bedroom slippers, then gets her shoes from under the easy chair and puts them on. She goes to the mantelpiece and pushes* HENRY *aside so that he sits in the easy chair.*

EMMA *takes a large bottle of aspirin from the mantelpiece, shakes out three tablets, puts them into her mouth, replaces the bottle and exits to the kitchen.*

EDIE, *a second later, enters from the kitchen like a bullet from a gun. She lands, quivering, above the easy chair.*

EMMA, *three seconds later, charges in from the kitchen, wiping her lips with her handkerchief.*

EDIE *immediately rushes off into the kitchen.*
EMMA *watches Edie go, as if unable to make up her mind whether to tread on her or not. She then gives a glare at all the men, and after a tremendous "God give me patience" sigh, she crosses and exits L, slamming the door behind her.* ALBERT *and* CARNOUSTIE *both heave big sighs of relief and almost smile at each other.* CARNOUSTIE *produces cigarettes and* ALBERT *lights them*)

CARNOUSTIE (*with a sigh of relief*) She's all right, thank God.

(HENRY *rises, removes his jacket and puts it on the back of the easy chair*)

HENRY. Don't count your chickens . . . (*He jerks his thumb towards the door* L) Delayed action—that's all *that* is. (*He sits in the easy chair*)

(*There is a few moments' silence and stillness in the room.*
EDIE'S *head comes round the kitchen door. She looks apprehensively around, sees that Emma has gone and teeters into the room*)

EDIE (*to the men; quivering*) Ooh! You *must* want a cup of tea, *now*.
HENRY. Edie, if you don't shut up about that bloody tea . . .
EDIE (*moving to* L *of Henry; whimpering*) Ooh, 'Enry! Don't swear. Don't call the wrath of Heaven on this 'ouse again. It's visited us once this morning, 'asn't it?
HENRY. "*Visited* us"? It's *lived* with us since the day I married it.
EDIE (*in torment*) Ooh, 'Enry! You didn't ought to speak of Emma as the wrath of Heaven.

(DAPHNE *rises and moves to the table*)

DAPHNE (*picking up Shirley's veil from the table*) Oh, my goodness!
EDIE (*to Daphne; desperately*) What's the matter? What's wrong?
DAPHNE. Nothing's wrong, Aunt Edie. It's just that Shirley's veil's a bit creased. It ought to be run over with a warm iron before she goes to the church—(*she looks roguishly at Albert*) again.

(ALBERT *winces*)

EDIE (*grabbing an end of the veil with both hands*) Give it to me, I'll do it.
DAPHNE (*firmly holding her end of the veil; apprehensively*) Well— Aunt Edie, Shirley did ask *me* to do it. It won't take me a minute.
EDIE (*almost mauling the veil*) No, no, let me do it, love. You've got enough to do, Daphne. You go and get yourself ready.
DAPHNE. But I *am* ready, Aunt Edie. Now you sit down and take it easy while you've got the chance.
EDIE (*twisting her end of the veil round her hands*) No, no. That's just what I mustn't do—sit down. I shall start *thinking* and thinking. (*She twists the veil*) No, let me do it, Daphne. It'll be something for me to remember—that I ironed Shirley's veil—the last thing I did for her before she was married.

DAPHNE. Look, perhaps I'd better . . . (*With horror, as she realizes what Edie is doing to the veil*) I'm *sure* I'd better.

EDIE (*looking and realizing; horrified and terrified*) Oh! *Ooh!* Oh, dear! All right, Daphne. (*She releases the veil*) *You* do it. I'll go and put the iron on. (*She darts to the kitchen door, then darts back*) Shall I take it in the kitchen out of sight? If Emma sees it . . .

(DAPHNE *looks ruefully at the veil then hands it to Edie*)

DAPHNE. It might be as well. But you will let me know the minute that iron's warm, won't you, Aunt Edie?

EDIE. Yes, love, I will. (*She looks sentimentally at the veil, then gulps*) Beautiful!

(EDIE *darts off into the kitchen*)

HENRY (*to Daphne*) You've got a nerve, Daphne, lettin' your aunt so much as 'andle it.

DAPHNE (*smiling*) Don't worry, Uncle Henry, I'll . . .

(*There is a minor crash from the kitchen*)

HENRY (*rising*) Wot the 'ell . . . ? (*He darts to the kitchen door and looks off*) Edie! What are you . . . ?

EDIE (*off; bravely*) I was reaching for the iron and I slipped.

HENRY. For Gawd's sake . . .

(HENRY *exits to the kitchen*)

DAPHNE. Never a dull moment.

(DAPHNE *looks towards* ALBERT *and* CARNOUSTIE, *who are sitting morose and glum. She smiles, then moves to the fireplace, looks in the mirror and titivates her hair*)

(*She sings*)   "Brightly dawns our wedding day . . ."

(*There is a slight pause*)

ALBERT. Nark it, Daphne.

DAPHNE (*chirpily*) I'm *sorry*, Albert, but if this is a wedding—give me a divorce.

ALBERT. You've got to have the wedding first.

CARNOUSTIE (*glumly*) Aye!

ALBERT (*suddenly and with vigour*) And we're having a wedding. Not a ruddy funeral.

CARNOUSTIE. I'd a'most prefer the latter.

ALBERT (*rising*) Carnoustie, are you a man or a mouse?

CARNOUSTIE. At the moment—a moose. And so are you.

ALBERT (*striding around*) What's the matter with us? Here we are —two able-bodied seamen terrified of one woman. It's bloody ridiculous!

DAPHNE (*smiling*) But it's true.

ALBERT (*firmly*) It's not true. I showed this morning that I wasn't frightened of her, and I'll show her again. This is still my wedding day, and I'm going to *enjoy* it. So are you, Carnoustie.

DAPHNE (*smiling*) But not in the same way, I hope. (*She sits on the pouffe*)

ALBERT (*suddenly*) Carnoustie, let me see you laugh.

CARNOUSTIE. Wha'?

ALBERT. Laugh, man, laugh.

DAPHNE (*to Carnoustie*) He means "Away, dull care." Ha! Ha! Ha! (*She looks at Carnoustie's morose face. To Albert*) Is that laughing? I don't think he can.

(ALBERT *laughs hysterically, crosses to the mantelpiece and stubs out his cigarette in the ashtray*)

ALBERT. Carnoustie, if you could only see your face.

(DAPHNE *and* ALBERT *laugh loudly at Carnoustie.*
SHIRLEY *enters quickly* L *and stands above the sofa*)

SHIRLEY (*half-terrified, half-angry*) Albert! Daphne! Have you gone out of your senses? If mother hears you . . .

ALBERT (*rushing towards Shirley*) Oh, my darling. You're lovely!

SHIRLEY. What? (*She evades Albert and crosses down* R *of the table*)

ALBERT (*down* L *of the table*) You're beautiful!

SHIRLEY. I'm just the same as I was a few minutes ago.

ALBERT. And as you will be for the rest of your life.

SHIRLEY (*in alarm*) Albert, you haven't been drinking, have you?

ALBERT. What, in this house? What a hope! No! It's my wedding day—and I'm happy.

SHIRLEY (*with a quick look towards the door* L) Oh, no, Albert. You mustn't be—not yet.

ALBERT. Come on, give us a kiss. (*He advances on Shirley*)

SHIRLEY (*dodging above the table; puzzled and frightened*) No, no. I've just done my face again. (*To Daphne*) What's the matter with him, Daphne?

DAPHNE (*with a look towards Carnoustie*) If a man told *me* to come and give him a kiss, I shouldn't stop to ask what was the matter with him.

CARNOUSTIE. You're shameless.

DAPHNE. Ooh!

ALBERT (*to Shirley; with outstretched arms*) I'm waiting.

SHIRLEY (*suddenly snapping*) Albert, I'm not going to do my face for the third time. (*She sits on the chair above the table*) For goodness' sake, let's sit down or something. Oh, if only it was time to go to the church and get it over with before . . . (*She is showing signs of "nerves"*)

ALBERT (*still determined to be bright*) Well, what do you know? Two loving arms outstretched and nobody to come into them.

DAPHNE (*rising and moving slightly towards Albert*) If it's an open invitation . . .

(SHIRLEY *and* CARNOUSTIE *rise*)

SHIRLEY (*sharply*) Daphne, do you mind?
CARNOUSTIE (*almost overlapping*) I don't hold with all this frivolity.
SHIRLEY (*almost at screaming point*) I can't stand it! I can't stand
it!

(ALBERT, *at once serious and alarmed, moves quickly to* R *of Shirley*)

ALBERT. Hey, what the . . . ? Shirl—darling—it's all right.
SHIRLEY (*urgently*) Kiss me, Albert. Kiss me.
ALBERT. But—your make-up?
SHIRLEY. Damn my make-up!

(ALBERT *kisses Shirley*)

CARNOUSTIE (*embarrassed and turning to go*) Perhaps I'd better . . .
DAPHNE. Hold your noise!
CARNOUSTIE (*turning*) What?
DAPHNE. And turn the other way. (*She looks studiously in the mirror* R)

(CARNOUSTIE *turns away and stubs out his cigarette in the ashtray on
the trolley* L)

ALBERT (*soothingly*) It's all right, Shirl—it's all right, my darling.
SHIRLEY. Albert.
ALBERT. There's nothing to worry about—not really.
SHIRLEY. Of course there isn't. I know that. It's just that—it's
been such a terrible morning and—and mother . . .
ALBERT (*swaying Shirley gently in his arms*) I know, my dear. But
it won't be long.
DAPHNE (*to Albert*) Can I turn him round now? (*She crosses to
Carnoustie*)
CARNOUSTIE (*turning to Daphne; indignantly*) If you were my sister
I'd turn you upside down over ma knee and give you a guid smack-
ing.
DAPHNE. Oh, why aren't I your sister. (*She tries to hug him*)
ALBERT (*with a laugh*) You'll leave Daphne alone, Carnoustie.
No manhandling her till after the wedding. She's a bridesmaid,
remember—with a job of work to do. And so have you, for that
matter.
CARNOUSTIE (*grimly*) Aye, I have. An' I'll do it properly, too.
Don't you worry yoursel', Shirley. I'll get him there this time if I
have tae drag him by the hair of his heid.
SHIRLEY. I wouldn't want Albert to marry me if he didn't want
to, Carnoustie.
DAPHNE (*with a smile*) Sez you!
ALBERT. I do want it, Shirl; you *know* that, but my God, I want
to get it over. (*He moves to the fireplace*) Look. How would it be if
Carnoustie and me were to slip out by the back door and go down
to the church now?

CARNOUSTIE (*eagerly*) Aye!

SHIRLEY (*rushing to Albert and clinging to him; terrified*) *No!*

ALBERT. But, Shirl . . .

SHIRLEY. You're not leaving this house until the very last minute, Albert Tufnell; not until the taxi comes to take you right up to the church door.

(DAPHNE *moves to the window and looks out*)

ALBERT. Don't you trust me, Shirl?

SHIRLEY (*grimly*) I trust you, Albert, but that's the way it's going to be. (*She looks at the clock*) And it'll be here—your taxi—in ten minutes.

ALBERT (*miserably*) A lot can happen in ten minutes.

SHIRLEY (*at once apprehensive*) What? What do you mean, Albert? Oh, Albert, don't frighten me. I can't stand it. Haven't I been through enough this morning? (*She weeps in Albert's arms*)

(CARNOUSTIE *sits on the chair* L)

ALBERT (*desperately comforting her*) It's all right, honey. It's all right. I didn't mean . . .

SHIRLEY (*brokenly*) I know you didn't, Albert. It's just that—I can't get this morning out of my mind—waiting in the church—thinking I'd lost you for ever. Oh, Albert. (*She sobs on his chest*)

(EMMA, *fully dressed for the wedding, and carrying her handbag, marches in* L. *She sees Shirley's distress, pulls up sharply, but merely stands watching, her face speaking volumes.* DAPHNE *and* CARNOUSTIE *look apprehensively at Emma. There is a pause*)

EMMA (*her voice suppressed but quivering with feeling; slowly*) I'm not saying anything.

(EMMA *crosses and exits to the kitchen.*
EDIE *shoots in from the kitchen and stands above the table*)

ALBERT (*moving down* R; *furiously*) Damn and blast! She *would* come in just then.

EDIE (*whimpering*) I'm sorry, Albert. I didn't mean to interrupt, but Emma . . .

ALBERT (*crossing to* R *of Edie*) I didn't mean *you*, Aunt Edie.

EDIE (*whimpering*) Oh, I thought . . .

(SHIRLEY *wipes her eyes*)

(*She sees Shirley. With great alarm*) What's wrong? (*She crosses to Shirley*) What is it? What's happened? Oh, you're crying. (*She weeps*) Oh, my poor Shirley. (*She moves to fling her arms around Shirley*)

ALBERT (*moving quickly between Edie and Shirley; desperately*) Oh, my Lord! Look, Aunt Edie, nothing's *happened.* Shirl, for God's sake tell her there's *nothing wrong.*

B

SHIRLEY (*in a broken voice*) There's nothing wrong, Aunt Edie. (*She dissolves into tears again*)

EDIE (*wallowing in anguish*) Ooh!

ALBERT (*almost shaking Shirley*) Shirl! Pull yourself together.

(SHIRLEY *continues to sob on Albert's breast*)

DAPHNE (*running to Edie and shaking her firmly*) Aunt *Edie!*

CARNOUSTIE (*rising and moving to the door* L) Well, if you'll excuse me . . .

(EMMA *marches into this near confusion from the kitchen and stands above the table. She carries a small piece of blanket.* CARNOUSTIE *stops dead.* ALBERT *and* DAPHNE *are aware of Emma,* SHIRLEY *and* EDIE *are not*)

EMMA. *Edie!*

(EDIE *almost leaps into the air and gives a strangled yelp*)

(*In a terrifying, calm voice*) The iron's on full tilt and it is red hot. Edie, can I ask you—I'm only *asking*, mind you—but can I *ask* you to go and do something about it?

EDIE. Oh! (*She moves towards the kitchen door*)

(EMMA *holds out the piece of blanket, displaying an iron-shaped hole burnt in it*)

EMMA. And can I ask you to take this with you?

EDIE (*taking the piece of blanket*) Ooh! I—I'm sorry, Emma—Shirley's veil—Daphne—I forgot . . .

(EDIE *exits to the kitchen.* SHIRLEY *sits on the pouffe. There is complete silence for a moment as* EMMA *takes up a commanding position up* L *of the table*)

EMMA (*in the same death-dealing, calm voice*) What's the time?

ALBERT ⎱ (*together*) ⎰ (*He looks at the clock*) Twenty to one.
CARNOUSTIE ⎰   ⎱ (*He looks at the clock. In a high, strangled voice*) Twenty to one.

EMMA (*looking almost accusingly at them*) Where's Henry?

DAPHNE. He went out into the kitchen, Aunt Emma. P'raps he's gone through into the yard to his ferrets. (*She sits on the left arm of the easy chair*)

(EMMA *is about to explode, restrains herself, and gulps*)

EMMA (*indulgently*) He's very fond of them ferrets.

ALBERT (*with slight trepidation*) Er—Ma—I . . .

EMMA (*turning to Albert; still calm-voiced*) Albert—d'you mind if I ask you not to call me "Ma"? It sounds common. (*With a large but evil smile at him*) Do you mind?

ALBERT. 'Course not, Ma—er—Mum.

EMMA (*after a slight pause*) What is it, Albert?

ALBERT. What?
EMMA. You were going to say something.
ALBERT. Was I?
EMMA. You were. P'raps you were going to tell me why Shirley's in tears again—a quarter of an hour before she goes to the church—for the second time. (*Again the smile*) Is that what you were going to tell me, Albert?
SHIRLEY. Mum, it really wasn't anything to do with . . .
EMMA (*chiding; with false coyness*) I'm talking to Albert, Shirley love. You mustn't interrupt.
DAPHNE (*rising and crossing to R of Emma; brightly*) Now look, Aunt Emma, surely it's natural for a bride to have a little weep—out of happiness?
EMMA (*with false surprise*) Oh, I see. How silly of me. Shirley's crying because she's so happy?
DAPHNE. Er—yes. (*She watches Emma and sits on the chair above the table*)
EMMA. So happy because Albert's going to marry her after all. Yes, it *is* natural she should cry, isn't it?

(HENRY *potters in from the kitchen. On seeing Emma, he turns quickly, hoping to get out again*)

(*She speaks without looking at Henry or giving any indication that she saw him come in*) Come in, Henry. (*Still the same "sweetness"*) Come and sit down a minute.
HENRY (*closing the kitchen door*) Well, as a matter of fact, I—I—I was just going to . . .
EMMA (*in exactly the same tone*) Come and sit down a minute.

(HENRY *sits on the very edge of the easy chair*)

Been out to see your ferrets, Henry?
HENRY. Yes—er . . .
EMMA. How are they? All right?
HENRY (*blinking*) Yes.
EMMA. That's nice, isn't it?

(EDIE *enters nervously from the kitchen*)

(*To Edie*) You stay in the kitchen and have a cup of tea, Edie.
EDIE. I've just 'ad one, Emma.
EMMA. 'Ave another, dear, and close the door after you.

(EDIE *backs out to the kitchen and closes the door*)

(*With a "smile" all round*) Now! (*She bangs her handbag down on the table*)

(*The others jerk and stiffen*)

(*Quietly and "sweetly"*) Your taxi'll be here in five minutes, Albert—yours and Carnoustie's. You did order them *again*, by the way?
CARNOUSTIE (*in almost a mumble*) Aye!

EMMA. Good! (*With a "laugh" in her voice*) I mean, it would be awful if there wasn't a taxi for him to go in now Albert *has* decided to go to church.

(*The others squirm*)

(*She sits on the sofa*) Five minutes—that just gives us time for a little chat. We don't want anything to go wrong this time. But it won't, will it, Albert? You've talked to me and put me in my place, haven't you?

ALBERT (*squirming*) Look, Ma—er—Mum . . .

EMMA (*"gently" but firmly*) No, Albert. Let me have my say first. I was in the wrong this morning. Everybody thinks so, so I must have been.

HENRY. Now, look, Emma, there's no need to . . .

EMMA (*chiding "softly"*) Hen-ry!

(HENRY *subsides*)

Whatever my faults, I'm not ashamed to admit when I'm in the wrong. (*She pauses slightly. With the "smile"*) So long as I *am*, of course. (*With brightness*) And now, I want to apologize to Albert.

ALBERT (*striding to* R *of the table*) What?

(CARNOUSTIE *sits on the chair* L)

EMMA (*magnanimously*) In front of you all I want to say how sorry I am for treating him so badly, and mistrusting him, and trying to domineer him and Shirley, and trying to come between them, and —and all the other things I'm supposed to have done.

ALBERT (*sweating*) Now, look, Mum . . .

EMMA. I apologize, Albert. There! I've done it. (*She rises*) And we'll say no more about it. (*She pauses slightly*) And now we've got other things to think about. Have you looked out of the window, any of you? (*She moves to the window and opens it*)

(*The sound of women's voices is heard for a short time*)

DAPHNE. We *have*.

(ALBERT *moves to the sideboard*)

EMMA. Seen all those women with nothing better to do than poke their noses into other people's business? (*She looks out of the window*) I see that Maisie Mottram's out there. She *would* be. Wait till the next time I find her cat on my geraniums. (*She turns*) Well, now—you all know as well as I do, that they're all laughing their heads off at what's happened. But when you go out and get into the taxis, you'll —I mean I'm *asking* you all—to just *scorn* them. We'll *scorn* the lot of 'em. (*She crosses to* L *of Henry and prods him. With just a trace of the old Emma*) D'you hear, Henry?

HENRY. Yes, Emma.

EMMA. We'll behave as if nothing had happened at all. We'll smile, smile and smile again. We'll try and make 'em believe we're all as happy as kings.

(EDIE's *head comes round the kitchen door*)

(*She sees Edie*) And we won't let Edie—(*she jerks her head towards Edie*) come as much as to the front door—that'll give us a *chance*.

(EDIE *withdraws her head. The sound of a taxi horn is heard off*)

(*She is galvanized into action and peeps out of the window. Not loudly*) That's it! That's your taxi, Albert. Where's your hat?

ALBERT (*picking up his cap from the sideboard*) It's here. Here's yours, Carnoustie. (*He picks up Carnoustie's cap from the sideboard and throws it to him*)

(CARNOUSTIE *rises, catches his cap and stands nervously twiddling it*)

SHIRLEY (*rising; tremulously*) Oh, Albert . . . (*She runs to him*)

EMMA. Now, now, Shirley. Remember what we agreed—smile, smile, and smile again.

SHIRLEY. Give me a kiss before you go, Albert.

EMMA (*crossing to the door* L *and opening it*) He can do that in the hall. (*She indicates the hall to Albert*)

(ALBERT *crosses and exits to the hall*)

(*She half-closes the door. To Shirley; urgently*) Don't you let him out of the house till Carnoustie's there, understand?

SHIRLEY (*nodding vigorously*) Yes, Mum.

(SHIRLEY *exits to the hall.* EMMA *closes the door firmly and stands above the sofa*)

EMMA (*urgently*) Carnoustie.

CARNOUSTIE (*nervously*) Yes, Mrs Hornett?

EMMA. Are you *sure* it's going to be all right?

CARNOUSTIE. All right?

EMMA (*with a jerk of her head*) Him—Albert. I mean he's going through with it this time, isn't he?

CARNOUSTIE. Of course, Mrs Hornett.

EMMA (*doubtfully*) H'm—well . . . (*Suddenly*) Have you got the ring?

CARNOUSTIE. Yes, Mrs Hornett.

EMMA. Were is it?

CARNOUSTIE. In ma pocket.

EMMA. Let me see it.

(CARNOUSTIE, *after a great struggle with his upper garment, produces the ring from his belt-purse*)

Put it away safely. (*She opens the door* L *and calls*) Shirley. You can come back now.

(SHIRLEY *enters* L, *crosses and looks in the mirror* R)

It's time you were beginning to get yourself ready. (*With a sudden thought*) Carnoustie!

CARNOUSTIE. Yes, Mrs Hornett?

EMMA. Don't you let Albert out of your sight till I arrive at the church.

CARNOUSTIE (*fervently*) Yes, Mrs Hornett. (*Quickly*) No, Mrs Hornett.

EMMA. Not under no circumstances whatsoever.

CARNOUSTIE. No, I promise I won't.

EMMA. Not even if he wants to . . . If he does—tell him he's got to wait.

(EMMA *puts* CARNOUSTIE *off* L *and follows him off*)

SHIRLEY. Daphne, my veil? Did you remember . . . ?

DAPHNE (*rising; with a gasp of horror*) Oh, my Lord! I'll go and get it—(*she mutters*) if it's still with us.

(DAPHNE *rushes off to the kitchen*)

SHIRLEY (*sitting on the left arm of Henry's chair*) Cheer up, Dad.

HENRY. Why?

SHIRLEY. Well, I'm not leaving the house *for ever*, you know.

HENRY (*muttering*) Blimey! If once I got away, catch *me* coming back.

SHIRLEY. Now you don't mean that, do you, Dad?

HENRY (*muttering*) I wish I'd the chance to find out. Listen, Shirley love, I'll give you a tip. If ever you're in doubt about anything and want your mother's advice—come to your father.

(EMMA *enters* L *and crosses to* C)

EMMA. They're in the taxi, anyway. So far so good. Shirley, where's your veil?

SHIRLEY. Daphne's gone to get it.

EMMA. And your bouquet?

SHIRLEY (*beginning to panic and looking around for her bouquet*) Oh! My bouquet. Where is it?

HENRY. Edie's got it out in the kitchen.

EMMA (*in the old voice*) *What?*

HENRY. She said something about giving it a drink of tea.

EMMA. Oh, Lord!

(EMMA *clutches her head for a moment then charges out to the kitchen.* HENRY *rises, collects his jacket and moves to Shirley*)

HENRY. Sit down, Shirley, or you'll be worn out *before* your wedding.

SHIRLEY. Oh, if only it was all over and Albert and me were on the train.

HENRY (*fervently*) 'Ear, 'ear! (*He crosses below Shirley to* L)
SHIRLEY (*smiling*) Would you like to be going on your honeymoon
again?
HENRY (*firmly*) No. I'd just like to be *going*.

(HENRY *exits* L.
DAPHNE *enters from the kitchen, carrying Shirley's veil*)

DAPHNE. Here we are.
SHIRLEY (*taking the veil*) Thank you, Daphne. You've ironed it
beautifully. (*She crosses towards the mirror* R)
DAPHNE. Glad you think so.
SHIRLEY (*looking curiously at the veil*) But—it seems shorter, some-
how.
DAPHNE (*almost grimly*) It is—somehow.
SHIRLEY (*aghast*) What?

(EDIE, *in a "state", dashes in from the kitchen to* L *of the easy chair*)

EDIE (*indicating the veil; in a whisper*) It *is* all right, isn't it? It isn't
ruined, is it?
DAPHNE (*brightly*) Of course not, Aunt Edie. Put it on, Shirley.

(SHIRLEY *puts on her veil*)

(*To Edie. Brightly*) Look! As good as when you . . . Better in fact. I
think it's improved by having a foot singed . . .
SHIRLEY. Singed?
DAPHNE. I mean—*taken* off it.
EDIE. It is all right, Shirley love? It was an accident. You see . . .
SHIRLEY (*turning and kissing Edie*) It's perfect, Aunt Edie. Bless
you. (*She looks in the mirror and adjusts the veil*)
EDIE (*whimpering*) Oh, Shirley, love. (*She dabs her eyes*)
DAPHNE. Now, now, Aunt Edie. "Smile, smile, and smile again"
—remember?
EDIE (*blinking*) What?
DAPHNE. Never mind.

(EMMA *enters from the kitchen carrying the bouquet and posy. They are
both dripping with water which* EMMA *is shaking off as vigorously as possible.* SHIRLEY *sees this in the mirror and turns*)

SHIRLEY. What . . . ? My bouquet! Mum, it isn't ruined?
EMMA. No, but it nearly was. (*She hands the bouquet to Shirley, then
crosses below the table, shaking the posy*)
EDIE (*moving to Emma; again in agony*) I thought they wanted a
drop of water, Emma, so . . .
EMMA. P'raps they did, but—they were just going under for the
third time. (*She flicks water off the posy into Edie's eye*)
EDIE. Shall I take them out and dry them, Emma?
EMMA. Yes, and put 'em through the wringer.

(DAPHNE *takes the posy then sits on the chair* L *of the window*)

EDIE. Yes. No.

MRS LACK (*off* L) Yoo-hoo! Are you there?

EDIE (*running to the kitchen door*) Oh, it's Mrs Lack from next door, Emma.

EMMA. Florrie . . . !

(MRS LACK *enters* L. *She takes life and other folks' troubles easily. She wears a highly coloured dress and a rakish hat for the wedding. She carries her handbag*)

MRS LACK. Yes, it's only me. (*With a broad smile*) Well, off we go again, eh? I'm all ready.

EMMA (*with great control*) Florrie . . . (*She stands below the sofa, half-turned away from Mrs Lack*)

(SHIRLEY *sits on the pouffe*)

MRS LACK (*crossing to* L *of the table; reproachfully*) You didn't tell me the wedding was on again, Emma. I was taking off me glad rags when I saw the taxi draw up and you pushing Albert into it, so of course I put two and two together.

EMMA. Did you?

MRS LACK (*cheerfully*) 'Course. So naturally I flew round and here I am. Congratulations, Shirley. You've managed to hook him after all, eh?

EMMA (*turning on her*) What?

MRS LACK (*to Shirley*) How did you manage it, love? (*To Emma*) It *will* be all right if I come down in the taxi with you again, won't it, Emma? It's a question of time, you see. By the time I'd walked to the Church the wedding'd be nearly over. That is, if course, if everything goes as it *should* this time.

(HENRY *enters* L, *wearing his jacket and bowler hat.* EMMA *gives Henry a cursory glance then crosses to the sideboard and picks up a clothes brush.* EDIE *darts into the kitchen*)

(*She waves coyly to Henry*) 'Ullo, Mr 'Ornett. (*She crosses above the sofa towards Henry*) "Once more into the breach, dear friends"—as Laurence Olivier said, eh?

(HENRY *crosses below the sofa.* EMMA *crosses and mets Henry* R *of the sofa, whisks his hat off his head and brushes it, scratches it with her nail, etc., while she speaks to Mrs Lack*)

EMMA. Florrie—if I can get a word in edgeways—come with us in the car by all means, if you must, but I'll say the same to you as I've said to everybody else if you don't mind.

MRS LACK (*blithely*) No, I don't mind. (*She sits on the sofa at the left end*)

(EMMA *replaces the hat on Henry's head, makes a dive at his jacket, drags it off his back, still without paying any attention to him, and gives the jacket a sound brushing)*

EMMA. Well, I've just been telling—that is—*asking*—(*she waves the brush at the others*) all of them—when we go out to the taxis to behave as if nothing has happened, see? To scorn all them friends of yours—(*she waves towards the window*) out there, and smile—smile happily, see? (*She shakes the jacket vigorously towards Mrs Lack*)

(MRS LACK *sneezes*)

MRS LACK. Oh, don't worry, Emma. (*With meaning*) I shall smile, all right.

EMMA (*after a quick glance at her*) Yes, and I hope it'll be the right side of your face. (*She helps Henry on with the jacket*)

MRS LACK ("*hurt*") Why, Emma, you know *me.*

EMMA. I *do.*

(HENRY *removes his bowler to inspect it*)

That's why I'm telling you. (*In the same breath*) Henry, we'll have that back where you found it.

(HENRY *quickly replaces the hat on his head*)

MRS LACK. Well, I will say this for you, Emma. You've never been afraid to speak your mind.

(EMMA *turns Henry to face up stage and brushes the back of his trousers*)

EMMA. Oh, no, Florrie. If *that's* what you think you're *well* behind the times.

MRS LACK (*gaping at her*) What?

EMMA. "Speak my mind"! (*She turns Henry and brushes his front*) Not me. Not in this house no more. I've been put properly in my place. It's as much as I dare to open my mouth. (*To Henry. Fairly sharply*) Foot up.

(HENRY *puts his right foot up on the right arm of the sofa*)

I've been shown the error of my ways, Florrie, and I've learnt my lesson. (*She tugs the turn-up of Henry's trousers down and a quantity of dust, matchsticks and a cigarette-end fall to the floor. In the same breath*) Edie! Dustpan and broom. (*She brushes the turn-up*)

EDIE (*off*) Yes, Emma.

EMMA. I'm not the Emma Hornett you knew an hour ago, Florrie.

MRS LACK. Aren't you?

EMMA. I am *not.* (*To Henry*) Other foot.

(HENRY *puts down his right foot and puts up his left*)

(*She repeats the business with the left turn-up*) No. I've learnt a thing or two since then. It seems I was a bully and a tyrant—whose only happiness in life was making other folks miserable. You didn't know that, did you?

MRS LACK (*hesitantly*) Well—er . . .

EMMA (*sweeping up*) No, neither did I. (*She finishes with the turn-up*) There! (*She puts Henry's foot down.* To Henry) Now, go and stand— (*she points to the fireplace*) over there and keep quiet.

(HENRY *crosses to the fireplace.*
EDIE *charges in from the kitchen with a dustpan and a long-handled broom*)

(*To Edie*) Give that to me.

EDIE. I'll do it, Emma.

EMMA. Oh, no, Edie. (*She takes the brush from Edie*) You sit down, Edie love. Sit down. Make yourself comfortable. (*She brushes vigorously*) It's time I started doing a bit of the rough work in this house for a change.

(EDIE, *dustpan in hand, unconsciously collapses on to the chair above the table*)

Perhaps that's the trouble. P'raps I haven't had enough to occupy my mind. (*She "sweeps" at Mrs Lack*)

(MRS LACK *rises, coughing*)

(*Fairly sharply*) Edie!

EDIE (*leaping up*) Yes, Emma?

(EMMA *points to the floor.* EDIE *at once flops on her hands and knees and holds the dustpan so that* EMMA *can sweep the dust, etc., into it*)

EMMA. P'rhaps if I'd had more business of my own I wouldn't have interfered so much in other people's. (*She hands the broom and clothes brush to Edie*) Get rid of these.

(EDIE *scrambles to her feet and exits to the kitchen*)

EMMA (R *of the sofa*) And who d'you think showed me I was wrong, Florrie, to take an interest in my nearest and dearest? It wasn't my husband who put me in my place, as you might expect—that is, if you can expect anything of him.

SHIRLEY (*rising; desperately*) Mum!

EMMA (*turning to Shirley*) And it wasn't my daughter . . . Shirley, there's something funny about that veil of yours.

(SHIRLEY *thrusts her bouquet into Henry's hand and turns to the mirror*)

SHIRLEY. What?

EMMA. It looked peculiar the first time you put it on. (*She moves below the table*) Not that it's any concern of mine, of course. (*She sees Henry with the bouquet*) And where d'you think *you're* going? Buckingham Palace?

(HENRY *quickly gives the bouquet to* SHIRLEY, *who sits on the pouffe.* HENRY *stands at the fireplace*)

(*She crosses to* R *of the sofa*) No, Florrie, as I was saying—it wasn't *my own family* pointed out my faults to me. I could have borne that. At least, the knife wouldn't have gone in so far. But no. They had to leave the job to a perfect stranger, if you please. Yes, and not only a perfect stranger, but a chit of a lad of twenty-four, an orphan—*and* a sailor into the bargain.

MRS LACK. Albert?

EMMA. No more. (*In a mutter*) And no less. (*She crosses to Henry and looks him over*) You should have a handkerchief in that pocket. (*She taps Henry's breast pocket*) . . .

HENRY (*about to move*) I'll just slip up . . .

(EMMA *gives Henry a little push to stop him going, then goes to the sideboard and takes a folded white handkerchief from the drawer*)

EMMA. You'll slip nowhere. Any slipping that's to be done in this house in future'll be done by me. (*She puts the handkerchief in Henry's breast pocket*) And that isn't for wiping your nose on. (*She crosses to* C) Florrie, from now on my name in this house is *mud*. (*She pauses*) Not so much as a chirrup will anyone get out of me; I'll just go quietly on, and look forward to the day when the wicked cease from troubling and the weary are at rest. (*She sits on the sofa*)

HENRY (*muttering plaintively*) Oi! Turn it up!

EMMA (*quietly*) Did you speak, Henry?

HENRY. Yes. I—er . . .

EMMA. You said something, Henry?

HENRY (*muttering*) Yes, but I wish I hadn't.

EMMA. This is your house, Henry, and if you've anything to say in it you'll be given a hearing. What was it you said?

HENRY (*reluctantly*) I said "Turn it up".

EMMA (*after taking a deep breath*) See what I mean, Florrie? I'm not allowed to speak at all now. I'm nothing in this house. Nothing. Just an empty syphon.

(*The front-door bell rings*)

(*She rises*) That's it. That'll be it. (*She moves to* L *of the table*)

(SHIRLEY *and* DAPHNE *rise.* MRS LACK *takes compact and lipstick from her bag and attends to her make-up.*
     EDIE *dashes in from the kitchen to* R *of the table*)

EDIE. The front-door bell, Emma. Is it the taxi?

EMMA (*quietly but firmly*) Edie 'Ornett. I've been accused of a lot today, but so far nobody's accused me of seein' through brick walls.

DAPHNE (*looking out of the window*) It isn't the taxi, Aunt Emma. It's a telegraph-boy.

MRS LACK. More good wishes for your future happiness, Shirley love.

EMMA. It's more than good wishes she'll need.

(*The front-door bell rings*)

Edie! That isn't a wedding bell that's ringing, it's the front-door bell, so—would you mind?

EDIE (*starting*) No, Emma. I don't mind.

(EDIE *crosses below the sofa to* L, *gets entangled with* MRS LACK *and exits* L. *We see that* MRS LACK's *lipstick has been smeared right across her face.* EMMA *picks up her handbag, crosses to the mirror* R *and looks in it*)

EMMA. Now, are we all ready, 'cos . . .

(*The sound of a taxi horn is heard*)

(*She indicates she has heard the horn*) Yes, and about time, too.

(EDIE *dashes in* L, *panting, and stands above the sofa*)

EDIE. Emma! The taxi! It's here. It's here. Emma!

EMMA. Oh, all right. We 'eard. (*She crosses to Edie and holds out her hand*) Give it to me.

EDIE (*blankly*) What?

EMMA. The telegram.

(*The front-door bell rings*)

EDIE (*starting*) Oh! Telegram.

(EDIE *darts off* L)

EMMA (*looking after Edie*) Well, Mr Albert Tufnell told everybody what was wrong with *me*, but it'd take the Queen's doctor and the whole of Harley Street to say what's the matter with '*er*.

(EDIE *enters* L, *carrying a telegram.* EMMA *puts her handbag on the table*)

EDIE (*triumphantly*) I've got it, Emma. I've got it.

EMMA (*to Mrs Lack*) See what I mean? (*To Edie*) 'And it over.

EDIE. It's for Albert. (*She hands the telegram to Emma*)

SHIRLEY (*moving to* R *of the table*) Oh. Shall I take it and give it to him, Mum?

EMMA. Please yourself, but I've *yet* to see a bride walk down the aisle with a bouquet in one hand and a telegram in the other. (*She opens the telegram*)

(EDIE *peers at the telegram*)

Edie! Take your nose out of it—(*she hands the envelope to Edie*) and get rid of that.

(EDIE *darts into the kitchen.* EMMA *glances almost casually at the telegram, then suddenly stiffens. She reads it again, and almost pales*)

EMMA (*after a pause; in a hollow voice*) My *God!*

(*The four following speeches are all more or less a panic-stricken babble and simultaneous*)

SHIRLEY (*at once terror-stricken*) Mother, what . . . ? (*She tries to snatch the telegram*)
HENRY. What is it? What's the matter?
MRS LACK. *Emma!* Nothing's wrong, is it?
DAPHNE. Aunt Emma!
EMMA (*evading Shirley's clutch*) No!

(*There is a moment of silence with* EMMA *standing quite still, then she moves to the kitchen door.* SHIRLEY *moves up* C. MRS LACK *crosses to* L *of the sofa*)

(*She calls hollowly*) Edie.
EDIE (*off*) Yes, Emma?
EMMA. Make a pot of tea.

(*There are gasps of horror from the others and cries of "Tea?" "But we haven't time." "But the wedding?" "What's happened?" etc., etc., ad lib.*

EDIE, *wide-eyed, enters from the kitchen*)

EDIE (*squeaking*) Emma! Did you say tea?
EMMA (*firmly*) I did.
EDIE (*bleatingly*) But, Emma—the taxi . . .
EMMA (*hollowly*) Tea!
EDIE. Yes, Emma.

(EDIE, *apprehensive and dithering, exits to the kitchen*)

(*She calls*) And, Edie——
EDIE (*off*) Yes, Emma?
EMMA. —put in two for the pot.
SHIRLEY (*frantic by now*) Mum, you can't do this to me. You've *got* to *tell* me. What is it? What does the telegram say?

(EMMA *slowly slips off her shoes, puts on her slippers and stands* L *of the easy chair*)

(*With a wild cry*) Mum! You don't mean . . . ? Oh, *no!*
EMMA (*her voice throbbing with rage and satisfaction*) Oh, yes.
DAPHNE (*incredulously*) Aunt Emma!
MRS LACK (*incredulously*) You mean the wedding's—off *again?*
EMMA (*sizzling*) That's *just* what I mean.

(SHIRLEY *sits on the chair above the table.* DAPHNE *hovers over her*)

HENRY (*helplessly*) I—I don't believe it.

(*All the "syphon" pose falls from* EMMA *now, and she becomes the*

EMMA *she always was. Lashing out left, right and centre, she bludgeons everyone into ultimate muteness as the scene proceeds*)

(*Weakly*) I don't believe it. (*He sits in the easy chair*)

EMMA (*bearing down on Henry; her voice quivering with low rage*) You don't *believe* it. You *don't* believe it. Listen to this, then, Henry Hornett—(*she flourishes the telegram at him*) and I hope every word burns its way into the heart you've never had.

SHIRLEY (*rising; almost hysterically*) What does it say? What does it say? Mum, you've got to tell me.

EMMA. I'll tell you all right, but Heaven help you when you hear it. You see, I'm trying to break it to you softly.

(SHIRLEY *gives a little moan of agony.* DAPHNE *tries to comfort her.*)

DAPHNE ⎱ (*together*) ⎰ Aunt Emma, you've got to tell her.
MRS LACK ⎰   ⎱ Yes, Emma, you've got to tell us.

EMMA (*surveying them all*) Very well. And, Shirley—I only hope you've got the strength to . . .

(SHIRLEY *wails*)

(*She reads*) "Able Seaman Tufnell. Care of thirty-three Cherry Tree Lane . . ."

HENRY. Yes, we *know* our address.

EMMA. Did you speak, Henry?

HENRY. No.

EMMA (*reading and giving every word full value*) "For legal reasons imperative you do not marry. Stop. Solicitor contacting you. Stop."

SHIRLEY. No! No!

MRS LACK. What does "stop" mean?

EMMA (*curtly*) Stop marrying.

SHIRLEY. Oh, Daphne!

(DAPHNE *puts her arms around Shirley and leads her to the sofa.* SHIRLEY *sits on the sofa.* DAPHNE *sits* L *of her*)

HENRY. But—who's sent it?

EMMA (*reading*) "Frederick Hardcastle. Lieutenant-Commander, R.N. Divisional Officer. H.M.S. *Hopeful.*"

HENRY. But—what does it mean?

EMMA (*fuming*) It means—(*in one breath*) for legal reasons imperative he does not get married. Stop. Solicitor contacting him. Stop. And if you don't know what *that* means, Henry Hornett, I give up.

SHIRLEY. I don't believe it.

EMMA. You've *got* to believe it. Far be it from me to add to your cup of bitterness, but you can make up your mind, this time, that you've well and truly 'ad it. (*She crosses down* R)

(EDIE *enters from the kitchen carrying a tray of tea*)

EDIE (*whimpering*) I've made the tea, Emma. (*She sees Shirley's distress*) What . . . ? Oh, Shirley, my lamb, my love, what's the matter?

EMMA (*with a loud cry*) Oh, don't you start. (*She crosses to* R *of Edie. In a voice throbbing with intensity*) Edie, give me that tray and get out of here.

EDIE (*pointing the tray towards Shirley*) But, poor Shirley, what's the matter with her, Daphne?

EMMA. Edie 'Ornett, with murder in my 'eart, I'm *asking* you to give me that tray and *go*. (*She puts the telegram on the table*)

(EDIE *almost hurls the tray into Emma's hands and exits to the kitchen*)

HENRY. But, Emma . . . (*He is like a lost sheep*) What are we going to *do*?

EMMA (*crossing to* L *of the table*) It's what we're *not* going to do that matters. (*She puts the tray on the left end of the table*) We're not going to a wedding—none of us.

HENRY (*desperately*) But we can't just leave it like this. There's Albert waiting at the church . . .

EMMA (*with fine scorn*) And what do you expect me to *do*? Run down there and take him a cup of tea?

SHIRLEY (*leaping up*) Daphne. Come with me.

(DAPHNE *rises*)

EMMA (*spinning round to Shirley*) What? Where are you going?

SHIRLEY. Where do you think? To Albert. (*She moves towards the door* L)

EMMA (*intercepting Shirley and blocking her way*) Shirley 'Ornett, have you taken leave of your senses? (*To Mrs Lack*) Florrie, pour me a cup of tea.

(MRS LACK *crosses, sits above the table and pours the tea*)

SHIRLEY. I've got to go to him, Mum. I've *got* to.

EMMA. You've been made a public exhibition of once this morning. Now you're going to make a laughing-stock of yourself again.

SHIRLEY (*sobbing*) I don't care. (*She sits on the sofa*)

(DAPHNE *sits* L *of Shirley on the sofa*)

I don't care . . .

EMMA (*interrupting*) No! You *don't* care. You don't care about all the shame and 'umiliation this has brought on *me*. (*With "tears" in her voice*) The fact that I've got to go on living in this street, and have everybody laughing in my face for months to come. No. You don't care about *that*—none of you. (*Her eye happens to light on the unfortunate Henry*) Look at *him*. (*She points to Henry*) *He* doesn't care. For two pins 'e'd 'ave his 'at on and be off to the pictures—*wouldn't* you?

(HENRY *puts on his hat and rises as if to go*)

Not now!

(HENRY *resumes his seat*)

MRS LACK (*holding out a cup of tea; timorously*) Your tea, Emma.

EMMA (*ignoring Mrs Lack; to Shirley*) And what will you do if you do go? Marry that man and be arrested as you walk out of the church? *And* spend your honeymoon in separate cells? A lot of satisfaction you'll get out of *that*.

SHIRLEY. Don't, Mum! Don't!

DAPHNE. Shirley, love . . .

HENRY (*desperately*) But somebody's got to go and fetch Albert. He's got to know. He's got to come back here and explain what that telegram's about.

MRS LACK (*a shade too enthusiastically*) I'll go. I don't mind. I'll just . . . (*She quickly drinks her tea*)

EMMA (*putting her hand firmly on Mrs Lack's left shoulder*) Nobody's going to the church.

HENRY. We can't leave that poor lad waiting and wondering what the devil's happened to us all.

EMMA (*crossing above Mrs Lack to L of Henry; with cold fury*) You *dare* say a thing like that. You *dare*! After what he did to us this morning. Kept us waiting half an hour and never turned up *at all*. None of you'll know what *I* went through—what I suffered. But— (*grimly*) Albert Tufnell's going to *know*. He's going to find out what it's like to have a church full of people staring at you until you feel you want to run screaming out into the street and let a bus run over you. Let him stay there! Let him stay and suffer. Then—when he comes back here he's going to suffer a lot more before he goes to gaol to suffer a lot more still.

SHIRLEY (*wildly*) No, Mum, no!

EMMA (*rushing to R of Shirley*) He's got to learn that he can't go about this world picking people up and trampling them down in the dust and get away with it *all* the time. (*She pauses. More grimly*) "The mills of God grind slowly, but they grind exceedingly small"—I'll see to that. (*She dramatically removes her hat and crosses to the sideboard*)

(*During the following speeches, which are spoken together,* EMMA *puts her hat and gloves on the sideboard.* HENRY *rises, and mutters as he removes his hat and jacket, then sits in the easy chair.*

EDIE *enters from the kitchen*)

SHIRLEY (*sobbing*) I don't want to hear any more, Mum, I can't bear it. If only you'd send for Albert.

DAPHNE (*trying to comfort Shirley*) Shirley, why don't you lie down quietly for a bit till Albert comes?

MRS LACK. There must be a reason, mustn't there? I mean to say, they'd never have sent that telegram if there wasn't, would they?

EDIE. You can't fight fate, that's what I say and I'll *go on* saying. When fate gets its claws into you you might as well give up.

EMMA (*turning*) D'y'mind? (*She pauses very slightly and crosses to* R *of the table*) D'y'mind, all of you, if—just for once—I'm allowed to hear the sound of my own voice?

Quick CURTAIN

ACT II

SCENE—*The same. Five minutes later.*

When the CURTAIN *rises, they are all in the same positions as they were at the end of Act I.* EMMA *is standing* R *of the table.* HENRY *is seated in the easy chair.* MRS LACK *is seated above the table.* SHIRLEY *is seated on the sofa.* DAPHNE *is seated* L *of Shirley on the sofa.* EDIE *is standing up* RC. *Chaos reigns. Everyone is talking at once. After a few moments,* EMMA'S *voice loudly tops all the others.*

EMMA. Thank you!

(The other voices die away)

(Quietly but firmly) Thank you very much indeed. For the last five minutes you've all been telling me what I *ought* to do—and I'm not going to do it. And now for a change I'll tell you what you're all going to do. For a start, Shirley, why don't you go upstairs and get out of them things? *(She indicates Shirley's wedding dress)*

SHIRLEY *(rising; vehemently)* No, Mum! I won't!

EMMA *(bristling)* Shirley . . .

SHIRLEY. It's all dreadful. I can't stand it. For two pins I'd throw myself in the canal.

EMMA *(crossing to* R *of Shirley)* Now then, now then! Let's have no more of that sort of talk. Throw yourself in the canal, indeed! No man's worth the sacrifice, and least of all—Albert Tufnell. Besides, that canal's a disgrace. I wouldn't throw a cat in it.

(SHIRLEY resumes her seat)

EDIE *(crossing to* R *of the table; wailing)* I understand how Shirley feels, Emma. *(To Shirley)* I know, Shirley. It happened to me, just as it's happened to you.

EMMA *(bitingly and reproachfully)* Yes, but *you* didn't throw yourself in the canal, *did* you?

EDIE *(whimpering)* No.

EMMA *(heavily)* No. And it was nice and clean in them days. *(To Shirley)* Well, if you won't go and get out of your dress, you can at least take that veil off. *(She removes Shirley's veil)* Here, Daphne. Take it upstairs and out of the way. *(She hands the veil to Daphne over the back of the sofa)*

DAPHNE *(rising)* Yes, Aunt Emma.

(DAPHNE exits L. MRS LACK *rises and moves up* C)

EMMA *(to Mrs Lack; indicating the window)* No sign of them two sailors yet, is there, Florrie?

MRS LACK (*looking out of the window*) No, Emma.

EMMA (*looking round for trouble*) Henry! Get that jacket on. We don't want the place looking like an old clothes shop.

HENRY. Albert'll have enough to worry about. Never mind what the place looks like.

SHIRLEY (*desperately*) Mum, you won't fly at Albert when he— when he comes, will you? Give him a chance to explain, won't you?

HENRY. Wouldn't it be as well if Shirley saw him alone first.

EMMA. Oh, no. Whatever explanation he's got to make he can make it in front of everybody. And Henry, when it comes to telling him we don't believe him, don't leave it all to me. (*She moves to* L *of the table*) Edie. You can get them tea things cleared away, and after that you can get yourself down to Banfields' Tea Rooms and tell them the reception's cancelled—again. And for *keeps* this time.

EDIE (*sobbing*) Oo-ooh!

SHIRLEY. But what will they think?

EMMA. They're paid to cater—not to think. Tell them I want everything—and I *mean* everything—packed up and sent round here right away. All the cakes—*and* the cake and the sandwiches— they needn't bother about the jellies and blanc-manges. (*With another sudden thought*) Oh, and Edie, you'd better take a basket down with you and bring enough food back for *us*. We may all be dying of grief and anguish but there's no need to die of starvation as well. Bring a good lot of the ham sandwiches—they're filling. You'll just have to put up with them, all of you. I shall have enough on my plate when Mr Alfred Tufnell gets here without cooking a hot dinner. Come along, Edie. Get a move on. (*She collects the bouquet and her handbag and puts them on the sideboard*)

EDIE (*picking up the tea tray*) Yes, Emma. (*She crosses to the kitchen door then stops and turns. Tearfully*) And, Emma, what about all the— (*she gulps*) the beautiful presents?

(SHIRLEY *gives a little moan*)

EMMA (*heavily*) The presents!

(SHIRLEY *whimpers*)

EDIE (*in anguish*) There are dozens of them.

EMMA (*practically*) Twenty-three.

HENRY (*blinking*) Twenty-three dozens?

EMMA. Twenty-three presents. They'll all have to be sent back. Nice job for somebody—packing that lot up.

EDIE. Yes.

EMMA. Yes. And *I* know who that somebody'll be.

MRS LACK. You needn't bother to send mine back, Emma. I'm sure Shirley's very welcome to it.

EMMA (*firmly*) That's very kind of you, Florrie, and we're very touched, aren't we, Shirley, but we've got far too much rubbish in this house as it is. (*She turns to Edie*) Now then, Edie, what about it?

EDIE. What about what, Emma?

EMMA (*patiently*) Getting them tea things cleared away and yourself cleared off to Banfields.

(EDIE *exits to the kitchen*)

EMMA (*calling to Edie*) See that all the presents are packed up and Henry will come down for them later, tell them. (*She closes the kitchen door*)

(SHIRLEY *rises and moves towards the door* L)

(*Sharply*) Shirley, where are you going?

SHIRLEY (*sobbing*) To get another handkerchief. This one is soaked.

(SHIRLEY *exits* L. EMMA *heaves a big sigh, collects a darning basket from the sideboard, puts it on the table and sits on the chair above the table*)

EMMA (*heavily*) Florrie, love. I don't know. I just don't know.

MRS LACK. What, Emma?

EMMA. Why this has to happen to us.

MRS LACK. *And* twice in one morning. It just seems as if it *had* to be, doesn't it?

EMMA. As if it hadn't, you mean.

MRS LACK. Well, that's what I mean, really; as if it *had* to be that the wedding hadn't, if you follow.

(HENRY *takes a pools coupon and a pencil from his pocket*)

EMMA. I don't and my head's going round and round quite enough as it is without working out crossword puzzles.

HENRY. Arsenal one, Chelsea—draw.

(EMMA *rises heavily, looks mournfully at Henry and speaks to him, not in anger, but with heavy pathos*)

EMMA. And, 'Enry, if only you'd be a bit more 'elp.

HENRY. Why, what can I . . . ?

EMMA. Well, look at you. Just sitting there as if you 'adn't a care in the world.

HENRY. I wasn't—I was just doing me pools.

EMMA. If you wanted something to read I should have thought it'd be this. (*She picks up the telegram from the table and thrusts it under Henry's nose*)

HENRY. But *you've* read this out to us, haven't you?

EMMA. Well, what if I have? You want to see it for yourself, don't you? I know I would.

HENRY (*taking the telegram; muttering*) Yes, *you* would.

EMMA (*after looking at Henry; to Mrs Lack*) You see, Florrie? *That's* what I have to put up with. A husband who won't face facts, and his sister who wouldn't know a fact if it come up and hit her in the face. And then people wonder why, if every now and again I get a bit cross.

(*Footsteps are heard off* L)

(*Suddenly*) What was that? I thought I heard someone on my stairs. (*She charges to the door* L, *opens it, and speaks off in a firm voice*) And where do you think you're going? (*Without waiting for a reply*) You'll come in here a minute, if you don't mind.

(DAPHNE, *now dressed in outdoor clothes, enters* L *and crosses to* L *of the table*)

Going out, eh?

DAPHNE (*firmly*) Yes.

EMMA. And may we ask where, young woman, or is it a secret?

DAPHNE. I'm going to the church, Aunt Emma.

EMMA (*with fine scorn*) To be baptized, I suppose? You'll stay here, my girl. (*She closes the door and crosses to* R *of the table*)

DAPHNE (*calmly*) Aunt Emma, I think it's about time you started wearing glasses.

EMMA (*blinking*) What?

DAPHNE. You must be getting a little short-sighted. I'm Daphne, not Shirley.

EMMA (*bristling*) What are you getting at?

DAPHNE. I'm just trying to make you understand, you're *not* talking to your daughter, that's all. If I want to go to the church, I shall *go*. And it just so happens that I want to go to the church.

EMMA (*aghast*) Daphne Pink! You dare talk to me like that!

DAPHNE. I do.

EMMA. Your mother's going to hear about this.

DAPHNE (*grimly*) She *is!* And *how!*

(SHIRLEY *enters* L)

EMMA. Shirley, have you put Daphne up to this?

SHIRLEY. To what?

DAPHNE. No, she hasn't. But my conscience has. When I think of that poor lad, standing in the church, being laughed at by everyone. *And* for something that's no fault of his own. It just scares me stiff, that's all. It's enough to make him . . .

EMMA. Scares you! Do you know what you're talking about?

SHIRLEY (*terrified*) Daphne! You don't mean you're afraid Albert will . . .

DAPHNE (*flaring up*) "Albert! Albert! Albert!" Damn Albert!

(*There is consternation from the others*)

SHIRLEY. Oh, Daphne!

DAPHNE. Who's talking about Albert?

EMMA. Well, you are, aren't you?

DAPHNE (*flaring*) No, I'm not.

SHIRLEY. Then who?
DAPHNE (*desperately*) Carnoustie.

(SHIRLEY *collapses on to the sofa*)

EMMA. What!
DAPHNE. Yes, Carnoustie. After all the humiliation he's had to
suffer today and what he's seen going on in this house, I wouldn't
be surprised if he doesn't come straight back for his things and catch
the first train to Scotland.
EMMA. For all I care, he can catch the one before. Nobody wants
to see him again.
DAPHNE. I do.
EMMA. What!
DAPHNE. Yes, I *do*. Like it or not, Aunt Emma, I do.
EMMA. I don't like it. I don't like it at all. It's disgusting and
shameless.
DAPHNE. There's nothing disgusting or shameless about it. I—I
think I love him.
EMMA. Love him! Well, if that isn't disgusting, I'd like to know
what is.
DAPHNE. Being in love with someone—disgusting? Of course you
wouldn't know. You've never been in love with anyone but your-
self.
EMMA (*low and threatening*) When your mother hears what you
said . . .
DAPHNE. She'll never forgive me for having said it before *she* did.
EMMA. Henry, did you ever hear such black wickedness? Me in
love with myself.
HENRY (*too reasonably by half*) I dunno. What's wrong in loving
yourself—if nobody else does?

(EMMA *opens her mouth to speak, then shuts it silently*)

DAPHNE. I'm off.
EMMA (*turning to Daphne*) I forbid you to leave this house. Your
uncle and I forbid it.
HENRY. I . . .
EMMA. Yes, you do.
DAPHNE. You can forbid till you're blue in the face, Aunt Emma,
but I'm still going. And I'll tell you something more. If Carnoustie
asks me to marry him, I'm going to say "yes". And if he doesn't
ask me, I'm going to make him ask me. And if I can't make him ask
me, I'll—I'll throw myself in that damn canal of yours—but not
until I've pushed *you* in first.

(DAPHNE *turns and exits* L. EMMA *crosses to* L *as if to follow Daphne*)

EMMA. Well, I . . . ! (*She stops and turns to Mrs Lack*) Florrie, did
you hear that?
MRS LACK (*with not entirely concealed satisfaction*) I 'eard!

(EDIE *enters from the kitchen wearing her hat and coat*)

EDIE. I'm going now, Emma.

EMMA (*firmly*) Good. You know *where* you're going?

EDIE (*blinking*) Banfields.

EMMA. Edie, there's hope for you yet. (*Sharply*) And what about the basket?

EDIE. Basket?

EMMA (*heavily*) For the sandwiches.

EDIE (*guiltily*) Oh, I—er—forgot.

(EDIE *exits to the kitchen*)

EMMA (*grimly*) I was wrong. There's *no* 'ope.

(MRS LACK *glances out of the window and gives a sudden yelp*)

Now what?

MRS LACK. He's *here*. He's coming down the street.

SHIRLEY (*rising and running to the window*) Albert?

EMMA. What? (*She moves to the window, puts Mrs Lack aside and takes her place. With satisfaction*) Yes, he's here all right. Guilt written all over his face.

MRS LACK. Written in large letters.

EMMA. And he'll come in here whining and pleading and grovelling . . .

SHIRLEY. You will listen to him, won't you, Mum?

EMMA. No 'arm in listening. In fact, I'll be very interested to hear what he's got to say. (*Sharply*) And you listen, too, Florrie.

MRS LACK (*fervently*) Oo! *I'll* listen.

EMMA. When we bring him to court you may be called upon as a *decree nisi.*

SHIRLEY. Court?

EMMA. And, Shirley, don't you go flinging yourself in his arms the moment he comes through the door, d'y'hear? No matter how much he whines and pleads and grovels, you're finished with him, you understand?

SHIRLEY. Oh, Mum! (*She moves and sits on the sofa*)

EMMA (*crossing to Henry*) And, Henry——

HENRY (*dolefully*) Yes?

EMMA. —you'll stand up to him and give him "what for".

HENRY. What for?

EMMA. You've always said you were the master in this house.

(HENRY *gapes, but says nothing*)

MRS LACK (*looking out of the window*) He's coming up the garden path.

(EDIE *enters from the kitchen carrying a basket*)

EDIE (*placidly*) I've got it, Emma—the basket.

EMMA (*to Edie; firmly*) Out!

EDIE (*blankly*) What?

EMMA. We don't want you . . .

(*There is a terrific door slam off* L)

Ooh, my front door hinges! (*She crosses down* R, *turns and faces the door* L)

(*The door* L *bursts open.*
    ALBERT, *wild-eyed, charges in* L)

ALBERT (*his eyes on Emma; yelling*) You bitch! You double-dyed bitch! (*He hurls his cap at Mrs Lack*)

(MRS LACK *fields the cap.* EMMA *shrieks with horror*)

SHIRLEY (*rising and rushing into Albert's arms*) Albert! Oh, Albert!

(ALBERT *picks Shirley up bodily and almost hurls her on the sofa*)

(*She screams*) Al-bert!

ALBERT. Sit down and keep out of this.

(*There are exclamations from the others*)

EMMA. He's off his head. He must be.

EDIE (*rushing to Albert*) Albert! Whatever . . . ?

(ALBERT *plants Edie firmly on the sofa,* R *of Shirley*)

ALBERT (*to Edie*) And that goes for you, too. (*He faces Emma across the table*)

EDIE. Help!

EMMA (*turning to Henry*) Henry! Do something.

HENRY. Now look here, Albert . . .

ALBERT. Whatever do you think you can do, Pop?

HENRY (*rising and advancing towards Albert*) Now, listen, son . . .

ALBERT (*threateningly*) You come a step nearer, Pop, and I'll stuff you up the ruddy chimney.

HENRY (*stopping*) Oh! (*He moves to the easy chair and sits*) Well, that's that.

ALBERT (*his voice throbbing with emotion*) Keep out of this, Pop. I know it's none of your doing. But I'm going to say a few things to this wife of yours and—I'm warning you, Pop—if you try to stop me I'll *do* for you. My God, I will!

EMMA (*almost gibbering*) You're listening to all this, aren't you, Florrie?

MRS LACK (*with delight*) I'm listening. (*She settles down on the chair* L *of the window*)

ALBERT. And I hope *you* are, Ma, 'cos I've got a hell of a lot to say to you.

EMMA (*bristling*) And I've got a . . .

ALBERT. Pipe down!

EMMA. What did you say?

ALBERT. Pipe down, and if you want it plainer—shut that great trap of yours.

EMMA (*yelling*) What!

ALBERT. 'Cos if you don't, I'll shut it for you.

EDIE. Ooh, Albert. You mustn't strike a woman. Not even Emma.

ALBERT (*to Emma*) You're feeling very pleased with yourself, aren't you, Ma?

EMMA (*fuming*) It's more than you *will* be, Albert Tufnell, when . . .

ALBERT (*sweeping on*) I'm an orphan, Ma. I don't remember my parents. I've always regretted that fact, but when I look at *you* I realize I'm the luckiest man alive.

EMMA. Now, listen to me . . .

ALBERT (*suddenly shouting*) It's *you've* bitched things up, isn't it? It's *you've* stopped Shirley coming to the church. You weren't going to let anyone get the better of you.

SHIRLEY (*rising*) Albert . . .

ALBERT (*shouting at Shirley*) You shut up!

SHIRLEY. Al-bert!

ALBERT. You and me are finished, see.

EMMA. I could have told *you* that.

ALBERT. And that's the way you've always wanted it. You've hated me from the first moment you set eyes on me. And not because it was *me*. You'd have hated anybody who wanted to marry Shirl, and for no reason whatever except that you are *you*. And you just love hating everything and everybody excepting Emma—bloody—Hornett.

EMMA (*quickly*) Florrie, shut that window—and write down what he says.

(MRS LACK *rises, closes the window, takes a small diary and pencil from her handbag, then sits L of the window and writes*)

ALBERT. Nobody but you would have done such a filthy trick as you have this morning. (*He suddenly shouts*) You never intended Shirley coming to the church, did you?

EMMA (*fuming*) She went there once, remember.

ALBERT. And I didn't—I know. But I had my reasons and I was man enough to come back here and tell you them—and we came to an understanding—you, me and Shirl. At least you fooled everybody that we had. But we hadn't reckoned with that maggity mind of yours.

EMMA (*shrieking*) "Maggity", Florrie—"maggity"!

ALBERT. God! How you must have laughed to yourself when you saw Carnoustie and me go off to the church, knowing damn well you'd got your daughter so much under your thumb you would stop her following us.

EMMA (*trying to get a word in*) Let me tell you . . .

ALBERT (*shouting*) You'll tell me nothing, Ma. There's nothing

left for you to tell. The last twenty-four hours I've spent in this
house have told me all I want to know. I'm getting out of the joint
just as soon as I've got my things together. (*He moves to the cupboard
under the stairs, takes out his suitcase and puts it on the sofa*)

(SHIRLEY *hovers ineffectually by Albert's side*)

SHIRLEY (*wildly*) No, Albert, no!
ALBERT. I've had my bellyful in this Hornetts' nest. In fourteen
days I'll be back on foreign service, thank God.
SHIRLEY. Albert, you can't—you can't go. Not just like that.
ALBERT. Can't I? Just any of you try and stop me. (*He collects his
raincoat and scarf from the cupboard and packs them in his suitcase*)
EMMA. Henry! Fetch a policeman.
HENRY (*rising*) What? I—er—I —Albert . . .
EMMA. Did you hear what I said?
ALBERT. What the hell are you talking about? This has got
nothing to do with the police. (*He closes his case, picks it up, then goes
to the cupboard and closes the door*)

(SHIRLEY *sits dazed on the chair* L)

EMMA (*crossing to the door* L) Hasn't it? We'll see about that. (*She
stands spread-eagled in front of the door* L *to prevent Albert leaving*)
ALBERT. If you've got to talk at all, for God's sake talk sense.
EMMA (*with quiet confidence*) You think you're clever, don't you,
Mr Albert Tufnell? But you've got another "think" coming to you.
You're not stirring a foot until we know the truth about you, and if
it's what I think it is you needn't bother about packing—(*she points to
the suitcase*) that thing, 'cos you won't want it with you at Dartmoor.
ALBERT. Dartmoor? I don't know what you're talking about.
EMMA. You don't, eh? Then read *this*. (*She sweeps dramatically to
the table and picks up the telegram, but finds it missing. In alarm*) Where is
it? (*She rounds on Edie*) Edie, have you . . . ? 'Cos if you have, I'll
brain you.
EDIE (*squeaking*) No, Emma. What?
MRS LACK (*quickly*) You gave it to Mr Hornett, Emma.
EMMA (*crossing to Henry and holding out her hand*) Give it to me.
HENRY. What?
EMMA. You *know* what. I gave it you to read.

(ALBERT *moves up* C)

HENRY (*fumbling in his pocket*) Oh. (*He produces a piece of paper*)

(EMMA *snatches the paper, turns to Albert and holds it at arm's length.*
ALBERT *puts his case on the floor up* C)

EMMA. You don't know what we're talking about, don't you?
Well, read that, young man, and perhaps it'll enlighten you.

(ALBERT *takes the paper and glances quickly at it*)

(*Triumphantly*) Go on! Read it out loud and then explain it if you dare.

ALBERT (*after a look at Emma; reading*) "Are your ferrets suffering from mange? If so Meggison's Mange Destroyer will . . ."

(EMMA *gives a yelp of baffled rage, snatches the paper and turns on Henry*)

EMMA (*choking*) You—you—you . . . ! Give it me.

HENRY. What?

EMMA. That telegram.

HENRY. Oh, the telegram. (*He searches his pockets and finds the telegram*)

EMMA (*snatching the telegram and turning to Albert*) There! Read that.

(ALBERT *takes the telegram and reads it*)

Well?

ALBERT. But—what does it mean? It doesn't make sense.

EMMA. It does to me.

ALBERT. Then you're a damn sight cleverer than I am; I tell you I can't make head nor tail of it.

EMMA. And you expect us to believe that?

ALBERT. Not *you*, I don't—no.

SHIRLEY (*rising hopefully; eagerly*) Albert! You *mean* that? You don't know what the telegram means?

ALBERT (*coldly*) I've said so, haven't I?

SHIRLEY (*doubtfully*) Yes, but . . . (*She sits disappointedly on the sofa*)

ALBERT. It's a mistake. It must be.

EMMA (*with fine scorn*) A *mistake*, is it? And what do you expect us to do now? Just say "Albert says the telegram's a mistake so let's all get on with the wedding and—and—Bob's Your Uncle".

EDIE. Oh, wouldn't that be wonderful! Oh, Shirley! (*She whimpers*)

EMMA (*rounding on Edie*) Edie Hornett! I thought I told you to get yourself down to Banfields.

EDIE. But, Emma . . .

EMMA. If you're not out of my sight in one minute, I won't be responsible for my actions.

EDIE (*leaping towards the door* L) I'm going, Emma.

(ALBERT *moves quickly to Edie and kisses her*)

ALBERT. Good-bye, Aunt Edie.

EDIE (*faltering*) You're not going, love?

ALBERT. By the time you get back I'll be gone. (*He retires to the window and studies the telegram*)

(EDIE *weeps*)

EMMA (*to Albert*) Oh, no, you won't, young man.

EDIE (*rallying*) 'Course he won't. He can't go without a sandwich, can he, Emma?

EMMA (*fuming*) You . . .

(EMMA *runs* EDIE *off* L *and follows her off*)

HENRY (*rising*) Tell me, Albert, is it true what you said just now, that the telegram's a mistake?

ALBERT. I tell you it *must* be, Pop. I just don't understand it at all.

(HENRY *and* ALBERT *move towards each other in mutual unease and meet below the table*)

HENRY (*almost gently*) But you do realize, don't you, son, why we couldn't let Shirley . . .

ALBERT (*quietly*) Yes. I realize. (*He reads the telegram; almost muttering*) "For legal reasons imperative—Lieutenant-Commander . . ."

MRS LACK (*to Albert; brightly*) 'Ere, 'ow many t's in maggity?

ALBERT. Two—what?

(*They all look balefully at Mrs Lack. There is a sudden uproar off* L, *it is* EMMA *and* CARNOUSTIE *in argument.* HENRY *moves quickly to the easy chair and sits*)

CARNOUSTIE (*off*) And what for why can I no' come in?

EMMA (*off*) Because I say so.

CARNOUSTIE (*off*) Mrs Hornett, I . . .

(EMMA *enters* L)

EMMA (*firmly*) I've said no and that's good enough, isn't it?

(EMMA *turns to close the door but* CARNOUSTIE *sticks his foot through and she is unable to close it*)

CARNOUSTIE. If you don't open this door in one minute, I'm going to gi'e it a push and . . .

HENRY. If he does, you'll probably find yourself in the middle of next week.

EMMA (*releasing the door and moving to Mrs Lack*) It's assault and battery—that's what it is.

(CARNOUSTIE *enters* L)

(*To Mrs Lack*) You're watching all this, aren't you, Florrie? You're my witness. I've told this man to get out of my house and he's refused. You've heard him, haven't you?

MRS LACK (*solemnly*) I heard him.

CARNOUSTIE. You've heard no such thing, wumman. (*To Emma*) There's nothing I want more than to get out of your house, but I'm not going without the property I left *in* it—property belonging to me and to Her Majesty's Government. (*He moves down* L)

EMMA (*fuming*) Then get your property, *and* the Government's and get yourself out of here, and you can tell Her Majesty from me that if you and—(*she points to Albert*) him's a fair sample of what she's got in her Navy, then my heart bleeds for her.

CARNOUSTIE (*derisively*) Aach, ye're a wicked owld bissom, and . . .

EMMA (*moving towards Carnoustie; threateningly*) Say that again—in English—and I'll sue you for libel.

CARNOUSTIE. Ho'd your whissht!

EMMA. Hold me what?

CARNOUSTIE (*crossing to Albert*) How's it going, Albert?

EMMA (*moving down L of the sofa; to Carnoustie*) Get your property and get out of here.

CARNOUSTIE. Not till I've said what I've wanted to say since the first minute I entered this house. (*To Albert*) And I don't mind telling you, Albert, that was the blackest moment in my life since the day I bought a packet of dirty postcards in mistake for views of the Firth of Forth.

ALBERT (*quietly but firmly*) Carnoustie.

CARNOUSTIE. Aye?

ALBERT. Pipe down, will you, for God's sake.

CARNOUSTIE. Pipe doon? (*Angrily*) No, I'll no' pipe doon. (*In horror*) Man, ye're not tellin' me ye've let them talk you round, are you? Man, I'm 'shamed for you. If you've no sense of dignity then I have. And I've been made to look a bluidy fool waiting in that church wi' a whole crowd of Sassenachs laughing their stupid heads off behind me back.

(ALBERT *hands the telegram to Carnoustie*)

What . . . ?

ALBERT. Read that.

CARNOUSTIE (*reading quietly*) "Able Seaman Tufnell . . ."

ALBERT. Not that bit.

CARNOUSTIE (*reading*) "For legal reasons imperative . . . ." (*With a yelp*) Albert!

ALBERT. You haven't finished yet. (*He crosses to the sideboard*)

CARNOUSTIE (*reading*) "Solicitor contacting you." (*Shocked*) Albert, what does it mean?

ALBERT. How the hell do I know? It's a crazy mistake.

CARNOUSTIE (*doubtfully*) Maybe—maybe. But Mr Hardcastle's a careful man. I should have thought he'd have made awfu' sure before he sent an expensive telegram like this. (*He sits R of the table and counts the words of the telegram*)

ALBERT. It's a mistake—it must be.

SHIRLEY (*to Carnoustie; tearfully*) Is it, Carnoustie, is it?

CARNOUSTIE (*doubtfully*) Well—I hope so.

ALBERT (*furiously*) What do you mean—you hope so? Don't you know damn well it *is* so?

CARNOUSTIE. I—I'm not saying anything.

EMMA (*moving up* L *of the table*) Aren't you? Then I am. You came for your property, young man. (*She points to the cupboard up* L) It's there. Take it and go.

CARNOUSTIE. That suits me fine. (*He rises*) Will you be coming, too, Albert? (*He moves to the cupboard and takes out his case*)

EMMA (*very firmly*) No, he won't. What, let him walk out and leave it at *that*. (*Loudly*) He's taken advantage of my daughter. (*She sits self-righteously on the chair above the table*)

CARNOUSTIE (*with great indignation*) He has not. (*He pauses briefly*) He's no' had the chance. (*He puts his case on the floor up* C)

EMMA. He's deceived her. Led her to believe he was free to marry her, knowing all the time that he wasn't.

ALBERT (*moving to* R *of the table*) That's a lie, I tell you. I didn't know. I still don't know. What are you suggesting, Ma? That I'm married already?

SHIRLEY. Oh, Albert!

ALBERT (*crossing to* R *of Shirley*) Look, Shirl. I swear I don't know what the telegram means. (*He goes down to her on one knee. Urgently*) You do believe me?

EMMA. Whether she believes you or not, she can't marry you, so . . .

ALBERT (*half turning to Emma; passionately*) For God's sake, Ma! (*He turns to Shirley*) You *do* believe me, Shirl? You don't think there's —there's another woman?

SHIRLEY. Another woman—Albert . . .

ALBERT. What?

SHIRLEY. You wouldn't say that unless—unless there *was* another woman.

ALBERT (*rising desperately and crossing down* L) Hell and damnation!

EMMA. Swearing won't help.

ALBERT. I'm not talking to you, Ma. I'm not listening to you. I'm not even *seeing* you.

HENRY (*muttering*) How's he do it?

ALBERT (*moving to* L *of Shirley*) Now look, Shirl, all I'm asking you to believe . . .

SHIRLEY. I don't know what to believe. After all that's happened today, I hardly know *how* to think. First you let me go to the church and don't turn up. Then when everything's straightened out—that telegram . . . I've been humiliated—I'll never be able to hold my head up again. (*She is getting hysterical*) I don't want to think. I don't want to believe anything. I just want to die.

HENRY. Don't we all?

ALBERT. Look, Shirl . . .

SHIRLEY (*leaping up and moving to* R *of the sofa*) Don't touch me. I hate you!

EMMA (*quickly*) 'Course you do.

SHIRLEY (*wildly rounding on Emma*) I hate *you*, too.

EMMA (*rising*) What!

SHIRLEY (*running to the door* L) Leave me alone! Leave me alone! (*She weeps*) Oh, Mum!

(SHIRLEY *runs off* L. ALBERT *sits despondently on the sofa at the left end*)

EMMA (*to Mrs Lack; quickly*) Florrie! Go in there and make a cup of tea quick, and bring it up to Shirley. (*She crosses to the door* L) And, Henry! You stay here and keep an eye on—(*she points to Albert*) him. Don't you let him leave this room, d'ye hear?

ALBERT. You needn't worry yourself, Ma. Wild horses wouldn't get me out until I know the truth about all this.

EMMA (*grimly*) Wild horses won't get you out when you *do* know it, either. It'll be a Black Maria.

(EMMA *exits* L. *There is silence for a moment as* MRS LACK *rises, busily puts Albert's cap on the table and moves towards the kitchen door*)

MRS LACK. Would you like a cup of tea, Mr Hornett?

HENRY. Tea? No, thanks.

MRS LACK (*looking at Albert and Carnoustie*) I don't know whether to offer you two . . .

(ALBERT *and* CARNOUSTIE *look at her but say nothing*)

No, I don't think I ought.

(CARNOUSTIE *sits* R *of Albert on the sofa*)

What do you think, Mr Hornett?

HENRY. I stopped thinking hours ago.

MRS LACK. My heart goes out to you, Mr Hornett. Nothing but worry and trouble, when all you ask is to be left in peace with your 'orrible ferrets.

HENRY (*at once alerted*) Ferrets! (*He rises and moves slightly towards the door* L. *Anxiously*) They ought to be fed. I ought to go and see to 'em, but—I wonder if I dare. (*He looks at Albert*) Albert, if I did just slip out and see to 'em, you wouldn't . . . ? (*He indicates "buzz off" with his thumb*)

ALBERT. 'Course I wouldn't, Pop.

HENRY (*with just a trace of doubt in his voice*) No. No, of course you wouldn't. I'll just go and see where Emma is.

(HENRY *tiptoes off* L)

MRS LACK. That poor man. He just can't call his soul his own.

(HENRY *enters* L)

HENRY (*a little brighter*) Yes—well—I think I'll . . .

(HENRY *crosses quickly to the door* R, *then suddenly stops and turns and looks towards* ALBERT *and* CARNOUSTIE, *who are not looking at him, then beckons conspiratorially to Mrs Lack and points upwards*)

Mrs Lack—you'll let me know if . . . ?

MRS LACK. Yes, Mr 'Ornett.

(HENRY *exits* R. CARNOUSTIE *glares at* MRS LACK *as she is obviously intending to stay and talk*)

Oh—the tea.

(MRS LACK *exits* R, *closing the door behind her*)

ALBERT. It's a "B", isn't it, son? A proper "B".

CARNOUSTIE (*grimly*) It's a "B" all right—wi' a lot of Hornetts thrown in. (*With a start*) Albert . . .

ALBERT. What?

CARNOUSTIE (*after hesitation*) Nothing, Albert.

ALBERT. What the devil do you mean—nothing. 'Ere! You've got something on your mind about this telegram, haven't you?

CARNOUSTIE (*miserably*) Aye. (*In a voice of doom*) Milford Haven.

(MRS LACK *gently opens the kitchen door and stands listening*)

ALBERT (*blinking at him*) Eh?

CARNOUSTIE. Milford Haven—Betty. Albert, when we put in to Milford Haven this last week, did you see her?

ALBERT (*puzzled*) See who?

CARNOUSTIE (*almost squeaking with anguish*) Betty Fisher.

ALBERT. Betty Fisher? Betty Fisher? Oh, you mean Betty Fisher. No, I didn't. Why should I?

CARNOUSTIE. Well, *I* did.

ALBERT. Did you now? You didn't say anything. How was she looking? She was a bonnie wee thing.

CARNOUSTIE. Albert—(*impressively*) she's no' so wee just now.

ALBERT. *No?*

CARNOUSTIE. No. And she won't be—for a few weeks yet.

ALBERT. What? Is she . . . ? You don't mean she's . . . ?

CARNOUSTIE. That's *just* what I mean. Albert—when I saw her— the day before yesterday it was—she asked after you—in a very curious tone of voice.

ALBERT. What?

CARNOUSTIE. Very curious. And in view of *that*, and the fact that Betty's the way she is, *and* that telegram arriving, I'm beginning to wonder . . .

ALBERT (*in a threatening voice*) What are you suggesting, Carnoustie?

CARNOUSTIE. I'm not suggesting anything. I'm remembering that night when you took Betty to a dance—eight months ago.

(MRS LACK *withdraws and softly closes the door*)

ALBERT (*rising*) What about it? You were there. And so was Toddy Wright.

CARNOUSTIE (*rising*) Aye, but we didn't see Betty home. You did.

ALBERT. But . . .

CARNOUSTIE. *And* you didna' come aboard till next morning. (*In his distress he crosses to the fireplace, leaving his cap on the table in passing*)

ALBERT. So that's the way your mind's working, is it? You know very well I missed the last liberty boat. (*He moves below the table*)

CARNOUSTIE. I remember that's what you *told* us—that you stopped the night at the Y.M.C.A. and I remember Toddy Wright thocht it verra strange at the time.

ALBERT (*accusingly*) And did you?

CARNOUSTIE. No, *I* didna'.

ALBERT (*crossing to* L *of Carnoustie*) But you do *now?*

CARNOUSTIE. I'm facing facts, Albert. I'm thinking aboot that telegram, and wondering whether perhaps Betty hasna' been along to see the Lieutenant-Commander . . . (*He breaks off abruptly*)

(MRS LACK *enters from the kitchen, carrying a small tray with two cups of tea*)

MRS LACK (*in a voice throbbing with satisfaction*) Ex-cuse me.

(MRS LACK *gives Albert a long look, crosses and exits* L. ALBERT *moves up* R *of the sofa as if to speed her departure*)

CARNOUSTIE (*looking after her with horror*) Albert. D'y'think she heard?

ALBERT (*moving down* R *of the sofa; blazing*) I don't care a damn whether she heard or not. (*Sweeping on*) But I'll ask you to remember, Carnoustie, that eight months ago I'd just got myself engaged to Shirley, here. And knowing *that*, you have the ruddy impudence to stand there and accuse me of getting another girl into trouble at that very time. (*He moves down* L) My God, Carnoustie, you've surprised me all right. You must have the mind of a sewer rat.

CARNOUSTIE (*moving below the sofa; furiously*) Say that again.

(*They face each other below the sofa*)

ALBERT. A sewer rat!

CARNOUSTIE (*furiously*) That settles it, Albert. That's too much. I've endured a great deal for your sake since I came to this accursed house. But to be told by my own shipmate that I have the mind of a sewer rat—that's too much. (*He collects his suitcase*) I'll be wishin' you guid-bye till the end of the leave. Impudent, I may be, but I hae ma pride. "A man's a man for a' that—an' a' that, an' . . ." Guid-bye, Albert. (*He picks up his cap*)

ALBERT (*moving below the table and turning away*) Guid-bye, and be damned to you.

(CARNOUSTIE *moves to the door* L *and turns, his eyes filled with misery as he looks towards Albert's back. He hesitates as if to relent and make up with him, but he suddenly stiffens and speaks determinedly*)

CARNOUSTIE. No! "A man's a man for a' that."

D

(CARNOUSTIE *exits* L)

ALBERT (*derisively*) "A man's a man for . . ." Oh, damn! Damn and blast everybody. (*He runs his hands through his hair, crosses and flops into the easy chair*)

(*After a moment the door* L *is kicked open.*
CARNOUSTIE, *case in hand, enters* L *and moves quickly above the sofa*)

CARNOUSTIE. Albert!
ALBERT. Changed your mind?
CARNOUSTIE (*wildly*) I canna get oot.
ALBERT. What?
CARNOUSTIE. The front door.
ALBERT. What about it?
CARNOUSTIE. It's lockit.
ALBERT. *What?*
CARNOUSTIE. It's lockit, I'm tellin' ye. And the key's no' there.
ALBERT (*rising; fuming*) She's done that. (*He crosses below the table to the door* L)
CARNOUSTIE. Mrs Hornett!
ALBERT (*fuming*) Couldn't even take my word . . .
CARNOUSTIE. How will I get oot?
ALBERT. There's the back door, isn't there?
CARNOUSTIE. Aye, there is—and I'm away through it.

(CARNOUSTIE *exits to the kitchen*)

ALBERT (*looking* L *and muttering*) God! If that woman was only a man—for just five minutes.

(CARNOUSTIE, *case in hand, enters from the kitchen and stands helplessly by the door*)

CARNOUSTIE (*squeaking*) The *back* door.
ALBERT. What?
CARNOUSTIE. It's lockit, too.
ALBERT. *What!*
CARNOUSTIE. Aye. There's no way oot. I'm defeatit. (*He puts his case on the floor up* C *and his cap on the table*)
ALBERT (*crossing to Carnoustie*) Do you mean you're just going to stay put?
CARNOUSTIE. What else can I do—wi' both doors lockit?
ALBERT (*derisively*) "A man's a man for a' that." What a man.
CARNOUSTIE. But . . .
ALBERT. The doors may be locked but there's the window, isn't there?
CARNOUSTIE (*his eyes opening wide*) Och—I never thocht.
ALBERT. I'll give you a hand. Come on, son. (*He moves towards the window*)

CARNOUSTIE (*stopping him*) Albert.
ALBERT. Well?
CARNOUSTIE. When I talked aboot Betty Fisher going to the
Lieutenant-Commander and blaming her trouble on you, I didna'
mean I thocht you'd be guilty of a dishonourable action like that.
Och, man, there's naething at a' to stop a woman making that
hideous insinuation aboot any man. But I'm sore afraid if there has
been an accusation against you, that bad old besom'll believe it.
ALBERT. There's nothing she'd like to believe better, Carnoustie.
Well, off you go. (*He gives Carnoustie a friendly pat on the shoulder and
moves down L of the sofa*)
CARNOUSTIE. Off where?
ALBERT. Bonnie Doon or Annie Laurie—wherever you want to.
You're a free man, Carnoustie.
CARNOUSTIE. But what aboot you? (*He moves up R of the sofa*) Are
you no' coming, too?
ALBERT. No. Not till I know what that telegram's about.
CARNOUSTIE. But, man! You may have to wait days. (*He moves to
the window and looks out*)
ALBERT (*striding to the fireplace; desperately*) But I can't—I can't
stay in this house another night. If I did, I think I'd end up by
murdering everybody in it.
CARNOUSTIE. Look, Albert, I noticed a nice wee hotel in the toon.
Let's away doon there and fix up for the night.
ALBERT. You mean for you, as well? But there's no need for you
to stay—spoiling your leave.
CARNOUSTIE (*earnestly*) I'm no' deserting you when you're in
peril.
ALBERT. Peril?
CARNOUSTIE. There's a hymn aboot "Those in peril on the sea"—
but the peril you're in on the land leaves the sea high and dry.
ALBERT. But I've done nothing wrong, man.
CARNOUSTIE. You're *alive*, aren't you?
ALBERT. What? Of course, but . . .
CARNOUSTIE. Then you're in peril. And I'm standing by you.
ALBERT (*with a step towards Carnoustie*) What's the name of this
hotel?
CARNOUSTIE. The Rose and Crown.
ALBERT. Right. (*He moves quickly to the cases*)
CARNOUSTIE (*opening the window*) Pass me ma things when I'm
through. (*He starts to climb out*)

(ALBERT *picks up a case, but has second thoughts and puts it down*)

ALBERT. I'll just make certain that . . . (*He moves towards the door L*)

(*As* ALBERT *approaches the door, it opens inwards. He almost unconsciously slips behind the door and holds it.*
EMMA *enters L*)

EMMA (*in great form*) What's this I . . . ?

(EMMA *sees* CARNOUSTIE *at the window. She dashes to the window, grabs him by the posterior and gives a tug which brings him flying back into the room. He ends up by the sideboard, while* EMMA *remains commanding the window*)

(*In suppressed rage*) I might have known. I might have known. (*She has her back to Albert*) And where's the other one? I suppose he's half-way down the street by now.

ALBERT (*stepping forward and letting the door swing closed*) Wrong again, Ma. He's here.

(MRS LACK *enters* L *with a squeak, having been hit on the nose by the door, and stands by it*)

EMMA (*turning*) Caught 'em just in time, Florrie. Clearing out like a couple of rats deserting a sinking ship. And Shirley said I had a nasty mind 'cos I locked the front door.

CARNOUSTIE. Look, Mrs Hornett, I'll gi'e you my woord that Albert wasna' leavin', that I was going on my own.

EMMA. And why were you sneaking out of the house?

CARNOUSTIE. Because I've the faintest suspicion I'm no' verra welcome *in* it. Indeed, I seem to recollect you've told me so once or twice today. (*He moves to the fireplace*)

EMMA. You can go—and gladly—but not before I've got a statement out of you.

CARNOUSTIE. Statement?

EMMA. Written, signed and sealed.

CARNOUSTIE. What aboot?

EMMA. Her! That woman at Milford Haven.

ALBERT (*starting*) What?

EMMA (*turning on Albert*) That takes the wind out of your sails, doesn't it?

ALBERT. Well, I've heard of walls having ears but I'd never have believed it.

CARNOUSTIE. Walls may have ears, Albert, but they can't run upstairs.

(CARNOUSTIE *looks at* MRS LACK *who casually picks up a magazine from the trolley* L, *and appears engrossed in it*)

ALBERT. Eh? (*He follows Carnoustie's look*) Oh, I see. (*He moves to Mrs Lack*) Yes, you're wired for sound, aren't you, Mrs Tannoy.

MRS LACK. I know my duty to my friends, I hope.

EMMA (*moving to* R *of the sofa*) Yes, Mrs Tannoy told me. And isn't it natural that she should? She has daughters of her own, haven't you, Florrie?

MRS LACK. I have.

EMMA (*to Carnoustie*) She heard you saying how he carried on with that girl at Milford Haven, betraying and deceiving my daughter. And I'm *grateful* to her for telling me. I hope I'll be able to do the same for her one day.

Mrs Lack (*putting the magazine down rather sharply*) What?

Emma. Where's Henry? (*She crosses to the easy chair*) He's got to know about this.

Mrs Lack. He's just gone out the back.

Emma. With them blessed ferrets, I suppose?

Mrs Lack. He did say *something* about—time they was fed.

Emma (*with a grand gesture*) I give up. I just give up. My last words to him were—don't you leave this room, and what's the first thing he does?

Albert (*quietly*) Leaves the room.

Emma. Who said that?

Albert. Me.

Emma (*snapping at him*) That's enough from you. We'll soon have him in here. (*She moves firmly towards the kitchen door*)

Mrs Lack (*crossing to Emma*) But, Emma, I . . .

Emma. Keep your eyes on them two, Florrie.

Mrs Lack. But, Emma, you can't . . .

Emma. If they clear out again, let it be over your dead body.

(Emma *exits to the kitchen.* Albert *perches on the back of the sofa*)

Mrs Lack. But, Emma . . . (*She shrugs her shoulders and turns*) She's a good listener so long as *she's* doing the talking.

Carnoustie. Och!

(Carnoustie *and* Albert *turn away from Mrs Lack*)

Mrs Lack (*bridling*) There's no need to be like that.

Carnoustie (*crossing to the sofa*) Ye're running with the hounds, woman. Leave the hares alone. (*He sits on the sofa at the right end*)

(Emma, *bristling, enters from the kitchen and crosses to* l *of Mrs Lack*)

Emma. Well, if this isn't the last straw. Not only does he go when I tell him not to, but he locks the door so I can't get out to bring him in.

Mrs Lack. But that's what I was trying to tell you, Emma. It was *me*. I did it.

Emma. Did what?

Mrs Lack (*producing a key*) Locked the back door—in case these two tried . . .

Emma (*grudgingly*) Oh—I see. Very wise, but . . . (*Rallying*) You don't want to make a habit of it, Florrie—playing fast and loose with other people's keys.

(Emma *snatches the key from Mrs Lack and marches out to the kitchen*)

Mrs Lack (*moving down* c; *dumbfounded*) Well, I don't know. There's gratitude for you. Ah, well. We live and learn,

(SHIRLEY *enters* L. *She is now in a skirt and blouse.* ALBERT *rises*)

Shirley, love, you shouldn't have come down. You should have stayed where you were and had a good restful sleep.

SHIRLEY. Sleep—after what I've just been told?

ALBERT. What? (*To Mrs Lack*) D'y'mean to say you let Shirley hear all that . . . ?

MRS LACK (*moving down* R) Truth will out.

ALBERT. You wicked old cow!

(MRS LACK *collapses indignantly on to the pouffe*)

(*He moves to Shirley*) Shirl, honey, there's not a word of truth in what you've heard.

SHIRLEY (*quietly*) Don't say anything, Albert, don't say anything at all—please.

ALBERT. But, Shirl . . .

SHIRLEY. Albert—I beg you. I've taken all I *can* take. (*Flatly*) There is a limit—there must be—to how much one can suffer.

ALBERT (*quietly*) You won't even listen to me?

SHIRLEY (*quietly and slowly*) No, Albert, I won't even listen to you.

(ALBERT *looks sorrowfully at Shirley for a moment or two, then turns away to the window.* SHIRLEY *sits on the chair* L. *There is a moment of complete silence and stillness in the room, then* EMMA'S *voice is heard in the distance, off* L, *approaching, and first* HENRY, *then* EMMA, *are seen passing the window*)

EMMA (*off*) And let me catch you with them blessed things again today and with my own hands I'll strangle 'em—I will, so help me God! Ferrets!

(EMMA *enters from the kitchen, pushing* HENRY *in front of her*)

You frighten me, Henry 'Ornett, you do straight. You think so much about them that you're beginning to look like 'em. There are times I wake up in the middle of the night and look at you, and without a word of a lie I wonder whether I'm in bed with a man or a ferret. Shirley! I thought I told you to stay upstairs? And have you brought the cups and saucers down with you?

(HENRY *quietly sits in the easy chair*)

ALBERT. For God's sake, Ma!

EMMA. I'll thank you to hold your tongue. (*To Carnoustie*) And I'll thank *you* to get that statement down in black and white, if you please. (*She moves to the sideboard, takes a Biro and writing pad from the drawer, and puts them on the right end of the table*)

HENRY. Statement? *Now* what are you talking about?

EMMA (*to Carnoustie*) In front of witnesses.

CARNOUSTIE (*rising and moving to* L *of the table*) Look, Mrs Hornett,

I am not committing to paper any words I may have had wi' my friend Albert.

ALBERT (*moving up* L *of the table*) Pipe down, Carnoustie. Listen, Ma. Whether you believe it or not, I'm *not* running away. (*Firmly*) And I've told you the *truth*. I don't know of any reason why I shouldn't marry Shirl. (*Quickly*) And I'm as anxious as you are to know what that telegram means. What's more, I'm not leaving this town until I *do*. I'm going to the *Rose and Crown* and I'm staying there until this is all straightened out. If you like you can send Pop down to keep an eye on me, but I am *not* staying here to be insulted by you or by anybody else. (*He pauses*) Have I made myself clear?

EMMA (*boiling*) You've made yourself . . .

HENRY (*rising; quietly but firmly*) Emma—they do say every man has one big moment at some time in his life—this is mine. (*He draws himself up to his full height and almost roars*) *Shut up!*

(EMMA *gasps and collapses on to the chair* R *of the table*)

(*He resumes his seat. Quietly to Albert*) Off you go, son.

ALBERT. Thanks, Pop. (*He collects his cap from the table and moves above the sofa. To Shirley*) 'Bye, Shirl. I'll be seeing you. Ready, Carnoustie?

CARNOUSTIE. Aye. (*He collects his case and picks up his cap*)

(ALBERT *and* CARNOUSTIE *put on their caps and move towards the door* L. *The front door is heard to slam*)

EDIE (*off* L; *excitedly*) Albert! Albert! (*To someone off*) Come this way, please. I'll tell him. (*More excitedly*) Albert! Albert!

(EDIE *dashes in* L *and holds the door open*)

Albert! Albert!

(*The others react in consternation*)

Surprise! Surprise! I found it on the doorstep. (*She speaks off*) Come in. Come in. He's in here. Albert, someone to see you. One of your shipmates.

(LIEUTENANT-COMMANDER FREDERICK HARDCASTLE, R.N. *enters* L. *He is a tall, bearded man of thirty-five with a rather commanding presence, and is in full uniform. He carries a brief-case.* ALBERT *and* CARNOUSTIE *both give a yelp, drop all their kit and, at once bring their hands up into a quivering salute.* HENRY, *flummoxed, rises.* MRS LACK *also rises*)

EMMA (*unimpressed by the uniform*) Well, if this isn't the very last straw.

CARNOUSTIE (*still at the salute*) Ma God, wumman, will ye no' hold your whisst. Do ye no' ken who it is?

EMMA. Stop jabbering at me in that heathen Scotch. If you can't speak civilized English then don't speak at all. (*To Hardcastle*) Now, young man . . .

HARDCASTLE (*moving down* L; *in a fairly thick Scottish accent*) I trust, ma'am, I have no' arrived at an inopportune moment, but . . .

EMMA (*rising; hearing the Scottish accent*) My God! Another 'eathen.

(HENRY *resumes his seat.* EDIE *closes the door and stands by it*)

HARDCASTLE (*to Carnoustie*) All right, Bligh.

CARNOUSTIE (*in a ringing voice*) Sirrr!

HARDCASTLE (*quietly*) Relax, Bligh.

CARNOUSTIE. Sirrr! (*He drops his hand but stands rigidly to attention*)

HARDCASTLE. I said, relax—*both* of you.

CARNOUSTIE (*in the same ringing voice*) Sirrr!

(ALBERT *and* CARNOUSTIE *relax.* EMMA *gives a little jump at each of the "Sirrs"*)

EMMA. Stop it!

CARNOUSTIE (*almost unconsciously*) Sirrr! (*He realizes it was* EMMA *who spoke. Ungraciously*) Och! (*He collects the cases and puts them tidily against the wall up* C)

ALBERT. I—I'm very glad to see you, sir.

HARDCASTLE. You received the telegram in time to stop the wedding?

ALBERT. As luck would have it—yes, sir.

HARDCASTLE. That's as well.

EMMA (*heavily*) If I may be allowed to put in a word in my own house—that is of course, if I'm not presuming—(*to Albert*) I should like to know who I'm entertaining.

ALBERT (*moving up* R *of the sofa; flustered*) Oh, I'm sorry. Sir—this is Mrs Hornett—Lieutenant-Commander Hardcastle.

(HARDCASTLE *crosses to* L *of the table*)

EMMA. Ah! It's *you*, is it? Well, perhaps we shall get the truth at last—not that we haven't got it already.

HARDCASTLE (*somewhat puzzled by Emma*) Mrs Hornett, I . . .

EMMA. This is my husband, Henry, Mr—er . . .

ALBERT (*moving to* L *of Hardcastle*) Lieutenant-Commander Hardcastle.

EMMA (*waving the fact aside*) Yes, well—as I was saying, this is my husband.

(HARDCASTLE *nods to Henry*)

HENRY. Pleased to meet you, sir.

EMMA. And that is my daughter, Shirley—poor girl.

HARDCASTLE. How do you do?

(MRS LACK *edges forward to* R *of Emma*)

EMMA. Oh! And this is . . . (*Quickly. With a cursory wave of the hand*) But she's neither here nor there.

(MRS LACK *retreats to the sideboard, bridling*)

Well, now we've got all the introductions over . . .

(EDIE *moves below the sofa*)

(*To Edie*) Out, you.

EDIE. But, Emma . . .

EMMA. I said "out".

EDIE. But, Emma, Banfields are sending the presents down right away 'cos they say they're cluttering up their tea-room.

EMMA. Then go and look out for them—anything, but get yourself out of here.

EDIE (*beaten*) Yes, Emma. (*To Hardcastle*) Pleased to have met you.

(EDIE *drops a curtsy to Hardcastle then crosses and exits to the kitchen*)

EMMA. And now perhaps we can get on. This man here can't marry my daughter. What's he done?

HARDCASTLE. I'd prefer to have a worrd with the able-seaman alone.

EMMA. Whatever you've got to say, you'll say—(*with a wave of her hand*) before this assembled company. We'll have no hole-in-the-corner-jiggery-pokery business, thank you. I know you sailors.

HARDCASTLE (*grimly*) I beg your pardon, ma'am.

EMMA. Come on, out with it.

HARDCASTLE. Tufnell, is it your wish that . . . ?

(ALBERT *shrugs and moves down* L *of the sofa*)

EMMA. Tell us straight out. Why can't he marry my Shirley?

HARDCASTLE. I repeat, this is no matter to discuss in public. (*He looks at Albert*)

ALBERT. Carry on, please, sir.

HARDCASTLE. Very well. With great reluctance then I have to inform you that the trouble is—a question of paternity. (*He moves above the table and puts his brief-case and cap on it*)

ALBERT		(*Alarmed*) What!
CARNOUSTIE	(*together*)	(*Alarmed and terrified*) No! Albert!
EMMA		You see!
SHIRLEY		(*She rises*) Oh! So it *is* true?

(*There are appropriate noises from* HENRY *and* MRS LACK. CARNOUSTIE *moves up* R *of the sofa*)

HARDCASTLE. Yes. (*He opens his brief-case*)

EMMA. Paternity. (*To Albert*) And you had the nerve to deny it; to swear to my daughter before the Almighty that it wasn't true.

Ooh—you. And now, out of—(*she points to Hardcastle*) your pal's own mouth . . .

CARNOUSTIE (*appalled*) Pal!

ALBERT (*frantically*) It isn't true, sir. I swear it! I don't care what the girl's told you. I took her home from the dance, I admit that, but as for anything else . . . I didn't even kiss her. Let alone . . .

SHIRLEY (*brokenly*) Oh, Albert!

HARDCASTLE. I don't know wha' ye're talking aboot. But wha' I'm talking aboot when I say it's a question o' paternity—I mean your *own*.

ALBERT (*blankly*) Sir?

EMMA (*sitting* R *of the table*) I can't *stand* any more of this. Mr Newcastle, for the last time, will you come down to brass tacks and tell me why Albert Tufnell can't marry my daughter?

HARDCASTLE. I will. Because—(*he points to Albert*) Albert Tufnell is *not* Albert Tufnell.

The others react. HENRY *and* EMMA *rise as—*

the CURTAIN *falls*

ACT III

SCENE—*The same. Immediately following.*

When the CURTAIN *rises, they are all in the same positions as they were at the end of Act II.* HENRY *is standing at the fireplace.* EMMA *is standing down* R *of the table.* MRS LACK *is standing up* RC. HARDCASTLE *is standing above the table.* CARNOUSTIE *is standing up* R *of the sofa.* ALBERT *is standing below the sofa.* SHIRLEY *is standing* L *of the sofa.*

ALBERT (*almost babbling*) Would you mind saying that again, sir?

EMMA (*looking hard at Hardcastle*) It's all that rum they get in the Navy—it does things to 'em.

(HENRY *takes his pipe and tobacco pouch from the mantelpiece, sits in the easy chair and fills his pipe*)

HARDCASTLE (*after a glare at Emma*) Naturally, I understand this must be a shock to you, Tufnell.

ALBERT. But—you just said I'm not Tufnell, sir.

HARDCASTLE. No, you're not.

EMMA (*heavily*) You're trying to tell us that—(*she points to Albert*) that *he* isn't *him*.

HARDCASTLE. In a manner of speaking—er—yes. You see . . .

EMMA. According to you I *don't* see. I think I'm seeing Albert Tufnell. You say I'm not.

MRS LACK (*moving down* R *of Emma*) You can't mean he's invisible!

EMMA (*firmly*) Thank you, Florrie, you've *said* your piece—d'you mind!

HENRY. Don't you think it would be as well to let—er—(*he indicates Hardcastle*) him say his?

HARDCASTLE (*gratefully*) Thank you, Mr Hornett. (*Generally*) What I hoped I had made clear is that—er—Tufnell's name is not really "Tufnell".

ALBERT. Then what *is* my name, sir?

HARDCASTLE. "Thimble." "Albert Thimble."

CARNOUSTIE. Ma puir wee laddie!

EMMA (*to Shirley*) See? Nearly got yourself married to a Thimble.

MRS LACK (*to Shirley; merrily*) And that *would* 'ave given you the needle, wouldn't it?

(MRS LACK *shrieks with laughter at her "joke" but subsides as she becomes aware of baleful looks from the others*)

EMMA (*sententiously*) Florrie . . .

MRS LACK. Sorry I spoke. (*She sits on the pouffe*)

ALBERT (*desperately*) I wish you'd explain, sir.

HARDCASTLE (*with a show of irritation*) I will, if I might be allowed
to—(*he produces a large file from his brief-case and waves it*) without inter-
ruption. (*He looks around at them all*)

(*The others are silent*)

Thank you. Do you mind if I sit down? (*He sits above the table and
takes some documents from the file*)

EMMA. Gather round, everybody.

HARDCASTLE. Er—Tufnell—Thimble—you've no objection to
this being discussed in—er—public? It *is* a delicate, intimate matter.

EMMA (*firmly*) We've got to know, 'aven't we? It's our rights. He
was going to marry our daughter and we want to know why he
can't. And we'll hear it from *you*, if you don't mind; not served up
second-hand by—(*she indicates Albert*) him.

(HARDCASTLE *looks towards Albert*)

ALBERT (*heavily*) Carry on, please, sir.

CARNOUSTIE (*moving to* R *of Albert*) Albert, if ye'd rather I went . . .

ALBERT (*moving up* R *of Shirley; quietly*) Sit down, son.

(CARNOUSTIE *sits on the sofa at the right end*)

MRS LACK (*brightly and insincerely*) If you'd rather *I* go, you've
only to say the word.

EMMA. In that case, Florrie, I'll say it. Go.

MRS LACK (*rising*) What?

EMMA. Go.

MRS LACK. But . . .

EMMA. Something tells me this is going to be all very embarras-
sing for me, Shirley and—(*she indicates Henry*) 'im. *You* wouldn't want
to be a witness to our embarrassment, would you?

MRS LACK. I'd be the last person . . .

EMMA. We understand, Florrie. (*Firmly*) Henry, see Mrs Lack *out*.
Where are your manners?

(HENRY *rises, takes a box of matches from the mantelpiece, and lights
his pipe*)

MRS LACK (*moving to the kitchen door*) I'm not one to stay where I'm
not wanted, but I 'ave been asked to two weddings this morning and
not seen neither.

(MRS LACK *exits to the kitchen, goes out of the back door and looks in
the window*)

Emma! I wonder if you ever *will* 'ave a wedding in the family.

(MRS LACK *looks towards Albert, laughs exaggeratedly then exits outside the window to* L. HENRY *is about to follow Mrs Lack*)

EMMA (*in a hoarse whisper*) Henry! Lock the back door.

(HENRY *exits to the kitchen*)

(*To Hardcastle*) I wouldn't put it past that woman to sneak in again and listen at the keyhole.

HARDCASTLE (*looking at his watch*) Mrs Hornett, if you *wouldn't* mind, I *should* like to deal with this matter and get away as soon as possible.

EMMA. I'm not going to be rushed. Shirley, sit on the sofa.

(SHIRLEY *sits* L *of Carnoustie on the sofa.* ALBERT *moves to sit with Shirley*)

(*To Albert*) You stay somewhere over there; as far away from her as possible, please. (*She sits* R *of the table*) *Now.*

(ALBERT *stands down* L *with his back to the trolley*)

HARDCASTLE (*heavily*) Thank you. I'm afraid this won't make very pleasant hearing for you, er—Thimble, but . . .

(HENRY *potters in from the kitchen and closes the door*)

EMMA (*sharply*) Henry, come and sit down. (*She indicates the easy chair*)

HARDCASTLE (*plodding on*) But you can console yourself with the fact . . .

(HENRY *sits in the easy chair*)

EMMA (*to Henry*) And don't interrupt.

HARDCASTLE (*gulping*) . . . console yourself with the fact that you are in no way to blame—that you are the—er—innocent victim of circumstance, shall we say?

EMMA. All right. We'll *say* it, and now let's get on with it.

(HARDCASTLE *slowly and deliberately puts a hand to his forehead, then runs it over his hair*)

Now what's the matter? Headache?

HARDCASTLE (*quietly*) No. Not yet. (*To Albert; with an effort*) You never knew your mother, did you?

ALBERT. No, sir. I was brought up in an orphanage.

HARDCASTLE. Quite. It's all down here in your records, of course.

EMMA (*exasperated*) Well, if it's all down there already, what are you doing . . .

HARDCASTLE (*also exasperated; his accent becomes more pronounced when he is excited*) Mrs Hornett, I am trying to make allowances for your —er—your unbalanced state of mind, shall we say?

EMMA. My unbalanced . . . What are you suggesting?

HARDCASTLE (*tersely*) I am suggesting that, at the moment, you are not your normal self.

CARNOUSTIE (*it bursts out of him; derisively*) Ha, ha, ha!

(HARDCASTLE *bangs his fist on the table*)

(*He leaps to attention*) Sirrr!
HARDCASTLE (*shaking his head wretchedly and slowly*) Relax, Bligh.

(CARNOUSTIE *resumes his seat.* HARDCASTLE, *almost baffled, puts both hands over his face. There is complete silence for a moment. All but* EMMA *are very embarrassed.* HENRY *gives a little embarrassed cough*)

EMMA (*sharply*) 'Enry!
HENRY. What?
EMMA. Quiet. (*Aside to Henry; with scorn*) Christopher Robin is saying 'is prayers.

(HARDCASTLE *pulls himself together and tries to smile*)

HARDCASTLE. Well, now. Perhaps with a little co-operation—(*to Emma; quickly*) but not too much . . . Now, where were we?
EMMA (*pointing to Albert*) Little Orphan Annie, 'ere, was being brought up.
HARDCASTLE (*gulping*) Quite.
EMMA. And at *this* rate, before we learn the truth, *we'll* all be in our coffins—being put down.
HARDCASTLE (*ignoring Emma*) Er—Thimble, I am sorry to have to tell you this, but you were born . . . (*He pauses*)
EMMA (*muttering*) 'Course he was.
HENRY (*firmly*) Sssh!
HARDCASTLE. . . . born out of wedlock.
ALBERT. *What?*

(*There is a rather sticky pause*)

SHIRLEY (*falteringly*) Oh, Albert.

(ALBERT *crosses below the sofa to* L *of Hardcastle*)

ALBERT (*quietly*) Is that a fact, sir? I mean, there's no doubt about it.
HARDCASTLE. There's no doubt whatsoever.
EMMA. Doubt! 'Course there isn't. I could tell there was something fishy the first moment I clapped eyes on him. (*With great scorn*) So that's what he is—a—a—yes, I'll *say* it—a . . .
CARNOUSTIE (*leaping to his feet*) Mrs Hornett!

(ALBERT *pushes* CARNOUSTIE *down on to the sofa*)

HENRY } (*together*) { Now, Emma, don't say . . .
SHIRLEY }   { (*Almost wildly*) Mum, don't—please!
CARNOUSTIE (*leaping to his feet*) Mrs Hornett! If you dare call Albert . . .

(*There is near pandemonium*)

ALBERT (*pushing Carnoustie on to the sofa*) Carnoustie!

CARNOUSTIE (*leaping up*) I'm no' going to let her or anyone else . . .

(ALBERT *pushes* CARNOUSTIE *on to the sofa*)

HARDCASTLE (*topping him; sharply*) Bligh!
CARNOUSTIE (*leaping to attention*) Sirrrrr!
HARDCASTLE (*firmly*) Relax, Bligh.
CARNOUSTIE (*glaring at Emma*) Is that an order, sirr?
HARDCASTLE. It is.
CARNOUSTIE (*quietly*) Sirr! (*He subsides on to the sofa*)

(*There is an embarrassed pause*)

ALBERT (*quietly*) Who was my mother, sir?
HARDCASTLE (*consulting his papers*) Er—a—Miss Rose Thimble—a spinster.

(*The front-door bell rings*)

ALBERT (*wandering to* L. *of the sofa*) 'Course—I—I never knew her, so—it doesn't matter a lot to me—I suppose.

(*The front-door bell rings*)

EMMA (*calling loudly*) E-die!
HARDCASTLE (*wearily*) Mrs Hornett—if I might . : :

(EDIE *darts on* R *to* R *of Emma*)

EDIE (*anxiously*) Yes, Emma? Is it all right? I mean—with Shirley and Albert? Are they going to live 'appy ever after?
EMMA (*heavily*) Are you deaf?
EDIE. No, Emma, but I thought you didn't want me to hear, and I'm not one to listen at . . .
EMMA (*heavier still*) The front-door bell. It's ringing.
EDIE (*listening*) Is it? I can't hear . . .

(*The front-door bell rings*)

So it is.

(EDIE, *laughing, prods Emma then runs off* L)

EMMA (*grandly*) I apologize for the—er—hiatus.
HENRY (*muttering*) Blimey!
EMMA (*to Hardcastle*) Well, I'm sure I'm very grateful to you for taking the trouble to come here and tell us the 'orrible truth. My husband's grateful, too. (*To Henry. Balefully*) Yes, you are. (*Smugly*) So now we know.
CARNOUSTIE (*rising to attention*) Sirr!
HARDCASTLE. You want to say something, Bligh?
CARNOUSTIE. Aye, sir.
HARDCASTLE. Could you not say it sitting down?
CARNOUSTIE. Och—but, sir . . .

HARDCASTLE (*tired of saying it*) Relax, Bligh.

CARNOUSTIE (*resuming his seat*) Sir. The fact that Albert is a—was —was born oot o' wedlock—that's no reason for forbidding the wedding, surely?

EMMA (*grimly*) Isn't it!

CARNOUSTIE (*rising; firmly*) Ma enquiry was directed to Lieutenant Commander Hardcastle, Mrs Hornett.

HARDCASTLE. Bligh, you're—(*he puts out a hand and waves Carnoustie back into his seat*) you're quite right.

(CARNOUSTIE *resumes his seat*)

Albert's illegitimacy—is not the reason for stopping the wedding.

ALBERT (*wretchedly*) What *else* is there, sir?

HARDCASTLE. The reason is more of a legal one. You see . . .

(EDIE *darts in* L *and rushes to* L *of Emma*)

EDIE (*as she enters; breathlessly*) Excuse me. Emma! Emma!

(EDIE *hisses at great length, with gestures, into* EMMA'S *unwilling ear, with scant regard for* HARDCASTLE'S *proximity*)

EMMA (*at last; irritably*) Well, go and fetch 'em *off* the doorstep.

EDIE (*breathlessly*) Yes, Emma.

(EDIE *turns, almost falls over Hardcastle and darts off* L, *leaving the door open.* HARDCASTLE *fumes*)

EMMA (*heavily*) I apologize for the hiatus.

ALBERT. You were saying, sir?

HARDCASTLE (*irritably*) What the dev . . . What *was* I saying? (*He glares at Emma*) Really, this is all very . . .

EMMA. Now then, now then! Don't give me none of your black looks. I 'ave a home to run. We're not all jolly Jack Tars, you know.

ALBERT (*quickly*) You were saying there's a legal reason, sir.

HARDCASTLE (*after gulping*) Oh, yes. Your mother, at your birth, took a step which was quite human and understandable, but quite *wrong* in law. She registered your birth under her own mother's maiden name—"Tufnell", instead of—"Thimble".

EMMA (*growling*) Jiggery-pokery—hocus-pocus.

HARDCASTLE. She had left her home sometime before your birth and moved to London where she lived as "Mrs Tufnell" until she managed to get you into an orphanage. Later, she married and, with her husband, she emigrated to Australia. (*He pauses briefly*) She died a year ago—a widow. London solicitors were instructed to make enquiries about her next-of-kin. Eventually, you were traced to your present assignment—the aircraft-carrier. The solicitors got in touch with the Captain, and . . .

(EDIE *charges noisily in* L, *staggering under the weight of a large card-board box which is filled to overflowing with wedding presents. She crosses below the sofa and table to* R *and hisses in Emma's ear*)

EMMA (*irritably*) Put it down.

(EDIE *puts the box on Henry's lap*)

Oh, not on him!

(EDIE, *with difficulty, picks up the box*)

CARNOUSTIE (*jumping up and crossing to Edie*) Here, Aunt Edie, let me help you.

(CARNOUSTIE *tries to take the box from* EDIE *and they stagger below the sofa*)

EDIE (*protesting and clinging on to the box*) No, no, Carnoustie, it's all right, thank you. I can manage. You sit down and talk to—(*she nods towards Hardcastle*) your friend.

CARNOUSTIE (*still holding the box; embarrassed*) Aunt Edie, the Lieutenant-Commander is no' ma friend.

EDIE (*distressed*) Oh, you 'aven't quarrelled?

CARNOUSTIE (*trying to take the box; more embarrassed*) Look, Aunt Edie—if ye'll just . . .

HARDCASTLE (*firmly*) Bligh!

CARNOUSTIE (*clinging to the box and standing to attention*) Sirrr!

(CARNOUSTIE's *leap up makes* EDIE *relinquish her hold on the box and she retires above the sofa.* CARNOUSTIE *stands rigid with the box in his arms.* HARDCASTLE *quietly rises, moves to Carnoustie, takes the box from him and, with dignity, carries it up* C, *puts it on the floor by the window, then resumes his seat*)

HARDCASTLE (*quietly*) Relax, Bligh.

(CARNOUSTIE *sits on the sofa at the right end*)

EDIE (*moving behind Hardcastle; ditheringly*) Thank you, sir, you shouldn't 'ave troubled, really. (*She bends confidentially over Hardcastle and without realizing it, puts a hand on his shoulder. Gently and indicating Carnoustie*) Why don't you and him make it up?

(EDIE *pats Hardcastle's head, then exits* L, *closing the door behind her*)

EMMA (*to Henry*) It's no use. She'll 'ave to be put away. (*To Hardcastle. Grandly*) Sorry for the 'iatus.

HENRY. Sorry for the what?

EMMA. 'Iatus.

HENRY. So do I.

(HARDCASTLE *examines the finger-nails of one hand for quite a time*)

HARDCASTLE (*to Albert; flatly*) The solicitors got in touch with the Captain . . . (*He looks towards Emma to make sure he is not going to be interrupted again*)

(EMMA *looks wonderingly at Hardcastle and then away*)

E

The solicitors got in touch with the Captain, and learning you were to be married today, said you should not be allowed to do so under a false name. The Captain instructed me to send that telegram, and suggested I might perhaps call to explain to you, personally.

ALBERT. It was very kind of the Captain, sir.

HARDCASTLE (*heavily*) It was—(*his eyes stray to Emma and he gulps*) *very* kind.

HENRY. It was kind of you, too, sir.

HARDCASTLE (*trying to muster a smile*) Not at all. I'm going on leave; it's on my way—besides—we—er—think a *lot* about—Thimble.

EMMA (*grimly*) I'm thinking a lot about 'im, too.

SHIRLEY (*rising and turning to Albert; falteringly and quietly*) Albert!

ALBERT (*turning to Shirley; quietly*) Yes, Shirl?

SHIRLEY. Albert, can you ever forgive me for . . . ?

(ALBERT *gives* SHIRLEY *a bleak smile and they give each other a small hug*)

EMMA (*alertly*) 'Ere, 'ere, 'ere!

SHIRLEY (*ignoring Emma; to Hardcastle*) But—er—sir ͅ ͅ ͅ

HARDCASTLE (*sympathetically*) Yes, Miss Hornett?

SHIRLEY. Does this mean that Albert won't be able to get married —ever?

HARDCASTLE. Good Heavens, no. But hardly today. You see, he has to decide whether he marries as a Tufnell or as a Thimble.

(ALBERT *is about to interrupt*)

Besides, there are certain effects—possessions—of your mother's and I imagine you would have to change your name back in order to claim them. And, of course, it was hardly fair—(*to Shirley*) to you, Miss Hornett, to allow you to marry without knowing the circumstances.

ALBERT (*eagerly*) But, if it's O.K. with Shirley, then there's nothing to stop us getting married right away, is there?

HARDCASTLE. If it's a matter of changing your name, I imagine that it would take some time.

ALBERT ⎱
SHIRLEY ⎰ (*together; dolefully*) ⎰ Oh, Lord!
                                    ⎱ Albert!

(ALBERT *moves* L)

HARDCASTLE (*to Shirley; comfortingly*) But perhaps your clergyman could obtain special permission.

ALBERT. Permission, sir? Who from?

HARDCASTLE. Oh—er—the bishop of the diocese, I suppose, or— (*he allows himself a smile*) perhaps the Archbishop of Canterbury.

SHIRLEY (*turning to Albert*) Fancy! The Archbishop of Canterbury.

EMMA (*in a flat voice; quietly*) Excuse me.

HARDCASTLE. Yes, Mrs Hornett?
EMMA. I've sat here very quiet. I haven't said a word. And no-body's bothered to say a word to me. But it's time I started asking a few questions. You say my daughter may have to have permission to marry 'im. (*She nods towards Albert*)
HARDCASTLE (*apprehensively*) Er—yes.
EMMA. And that the Archbishop of Canterbury will give it to her?
HARDCASTLE (*smiling*) Well, I was only . . .
EMMA (*with heavy sarcasm*) It seems I've been living under a mis-appre'ension all these years. I thought *I* was Shirley's mother—not the Archbishop of Canterbury.
HARDCASTLE (*after blinking at Emma*) What?
SHIRLEY. Mum . . .
EMMA (*quietly but firmly*) If I say Shirley won't marry this—er—Thimble—she won't. And I say that with all due respect to the Archbishop of Canterbury, the Dean of St Paul's and the entire Roman Catholic Vatican.

(*There are the beginnings of a hubbub*)

CARNOUSTIE (*rising*) Mrs Hornett, ye canna stop the wedding now.
HARDCASTLE. But, Mrs Hornett, you don't mean to tell me that because Albert is not—er . . .
EMMA (*quietly but firmly*) I don't mean to tell *you* anything, my lad.
CARNOUSTIE. "Ma lad!" Oh, my God! (*He resumes his seat*)
EMMA (*rising and standing up R of the table; to Hardcastle*) You may have a beard, and you may be a little king in your boat——

(*There are reactionary winces from* HARDCASTLE *and* CARNOUSTIE)

—pacing your forequarters with everyone raising their hats to you, but here—you're of no more importance than . . . (*She looks around to complete the phrase and her arm goes out, pointing to Henry. She does not say the word "him". She is obviously about to do so, but allows the gesture to speak for the word. She gives a little throat-clearing cough then turns to Hard-castle*) See what I mean?
HARDCASTLE (*indignantly*) Mrs Hornett . . . (*He packs up his papers*)
EMMA (*inexorably*) You came to say what you had to say and you've said it and, as far as I can see, there's nothing more for you to *say*. Whatever's said now will be said privately between *me* and—(*she points to Albert*) 'im. So—(*she makes a hinting "breaking-up-the-party" move with her chair, and crosses to the mirror R*) if you don't mind . . .

(HARDCASTLE, *after a long look at Emma, slowly rises.* CARNOUSTIE *and* ALBERT *stand to attention.* CARNOUSTIE *stamping loudly.* HENRY *automatically rises and stands rigidly to attention*)

(*She looks at Henry*) What are you standing like that for?
HENRY. Well—er—the Lieutenant-Commander's just going.

EMMA (*derisively*) And what are *you* going to do—pipe him overboard? (*She turns to the mirror*)

(HARDCASTLE *picks up his brief-case and moves towards the door* L)

ALBERT (*moving and meeting Hardcastle above the sofa*) There's nothing else you have to say, sir?

(SHIRLEY *sits on the sofa.* CARNOUSTIE *marches noisily to the door* L) *punctuating Hardcastle's speech with loud stamps*)

HARDCASTLE. There's a lot I'd like to say, but—I left my car— I left—I left—(*he glares at Carnoustie*) my car in the market square. You'd better walk down there with me.

(CARNOUSTIE *opens the door and stands above it.* EDIE *enters* L, *carrying her basket*)

EDIE (*crossing to the sideboard; brightly*) All over and done with? (*She takes a large quantity of sandwiches, wrapped in greaseproof paper, from her basket and puts some of them on a plate*)

(SHIRLEY *rises and moves* R *of the sofa and stands between Albert and Hardcastle.* EMMA *is busying herself at the mantelpiece*)

SHIRLEY (*to Hardcastle; genuinely*) Thank you, sir, for all the trouble you've been to and—(*she looks towards Emma's back; quietly*) I'm sorry mother's . . .

(HARDCASTLE *smiles understandingly at Shirley*)

(*To Albert*) You'll—you'll be coming back, won't you, Albert?

ALBERT (*smiling*) 'Course I will. (*He moves to take Shirley in his arms, but, aware of Hardcastle, refrains from doing so*)

SHIRLEY. Good-bye, sir.

HARDCASTLE (*shaking hands with Shirley*) Good-bye, Miss Hornett. I'm sure you'll have a very happy married life.

SHIRLEY. Thank you, sir.

EDIE (*moving* C *with the plate of sandwiches*) Oh—you mean they're going to be married?

EMMA (*turning to Edie*) Edie, quiet!

(SHIRLEY *exits* L)

HARDCASTLE (*looking at his watch*) I must ring the Captain to say "mission completed" so I'll away.

EDIE. You're not going?

HARDCASTLE. I am.

EDIE (*moving to* R *of Hardcastle*) But you can't—you 'aven't 'ad a sandwich. Won't you take one?

HARDCASTLE (*grimly*) I've had all I can take this morning, thank you.

EDIE. Shall I wrap some up for you?

EMMA. Edie, put them sandwiches down and get that lot—(*she points to the box of presents*) unpacked.

(EDIE *puts the sandwiches on the table then takes some presents from the cardboard box and puts them on the chair* L *of the window*)

CARNOUSTIE (*still holding the door*) Albert, wha' aboot me? Ye're no' going to leave me here, are you?

HARDCASTLE. Bligh!

CARNOUSTIE. Sirr!

HARDCASTLE. There are one or two things I'd like to say alone to—Thimble.

CARNOUSTIE. Sirr!

HARDCASTLE. And, Bligh . . .

(DAPHNE *enters* L *and stands* L *of Carnoustie*)

DAPHNE (*to Carnoustie; not too pleased*) Oh, *there* you are. I've been looking everywhere for *you*.

CARNOUSTIE (*horrified that she has interrupted Hardcastle*) Daphne!

DAPHNE. And don't stick your chest out to me. (*She gives Carnoustie a sharp dig in the stomach*)

CARNOUSTIE (*collapsing, very undignified, and holding his stomach*) Ouch!

DAPHNE (*noticing Hardcastle and whispering to Carnoustie*) Ooh, who's—(*she nods towards Hardcastle*) the Admiral? Aren't you going to introduce me?

CARNOUSTIE (*hissing at Daphne*) Ho'd your whist.

(EDIE *takes a cardboard box with a lampshade in it from the box of presents*)

Do ye want me clappit in irons for the rest o' ma life?

(DAPHNE *sits on the chair* L)

HARDCASTLE (*to Albert*) Are you ready?

ALBERT. Yessir.

(EDIE *takes the lampshade from its box*)

HARDCASTLE. Right. Oh—my cap. (*He moves to* L *of Edie at the table*)

(EDIE *unconsciously thrusts the lampshade into Hardcastle's hand*)

(*With his mind on Emma, he automatically takes the shade from Edie*) Thank you. (*He sweeps the shade on to his head, marches to the door* L, *then realizes his mistake and throws the shade furiously to the ground*) Tchah! (*He collects his cap from the table, puts it on and sternly salutes*) Good day, Bligh.

CARNOUSTIE (*saluting*) Sirr!

HARDCASTLE (*to Henry*) Mr Hornett . . .

HENRY (*copying Carnoustie and saluting automatically*) Sir!

HARDCASTLE (*somewhat coldly*) Mrs Hornett . . .

(EMMA, *not realizing what she is doing, leaps to attention and salutes*)

EMMA. Sir!

HARDCASTLE (*after looking at Emma for one brief moment*) Relax, Mrs Hornett.

(HARDCASTLE *exits* L.

ALBERT *follows him off.* EDIE *collects the shade and puts it with the other presents*)

EMMA (*realizing what she has done; furiously*) Ooooh!

CARNOUSTIE (*falteringly*) I'll—I'll—just go and see them to the door.

DAPHNE (*rising; firmly*) Not without me.

(CARNOUSTIE *exits* L.

DAPHNE *follows him off.* EDIE *unpacks a small statuette*)

EMMA (*moving up* C; *furiously*) I could brain you, Henry Hornett.

HENRY. Why, what have I done?

EMMA. Making me call that man "sir".

HENRY. But I was only trying to help.

EMMA. Edie. What are you standing there looking so pleased about?

EDIE (*twisting the statuette in her hands*) Oooh! Isn't it wonderful!

EMMA (*looking at the statuette*) Six and eleven at Marks and Spencers. (*She crosses to the sideboard and looks in the drawers*)

(HENRY *sits in the easy chair*)

EDIE. I meant Shirley and Albert. Everything's come right. (*With a big sigh*) Love has found a way. (*She twists the statuette still more*)

EMMA (*fuming*) Love has . . . !

EDIE. Isn't it wonderful? After all that's 'appened those two have come together again. (*The statuette breaks in her hands*) Ooh! (*She holds out the pieces*)

EMMA (*snatching the pieces from Edie*) Edie Hornett, will you—just for once—(*she puts the pieces of statuette in the sideboard drawer*) take yourself out of my sight for five minutes—five heavenly minutes—until I get things sorted out in Henry's mind?

EDIE. Well, what can I do?

EMMA. Don't ask me.

EDIE. I know. I know what I'll do. (*She darts to the door* L)

EMMA (*suddenly alarmed*) Don't you dare.

EDIE. But you don't know what it is.

EMMA. Whatever it is, it'll mean another headache for me.

EDIE (*gaily*) Not this time, Emma—this'll make *everybody* happy.

EMMA. Will it, now? Well, if you *should* happen to be thinking about the canal at last, Edie, you might take that cat of Maisie Mottram's with you. (*Firmly*) Out!

(EDIE *exits* L. HENRY *lights his pipe*)

HENRY. Well, that's that. And now what?

EMMA (*sitting above the table and starting to darn a sock*) We've got to think.

HENRY. Have we?

EMMA. We have. And I suppose as usual I'll have to think for you.

HENRY. And what are you going to think for me about? As far as I can see everything's hunkey-dory, ship-shape and Bristol fashion. (*He mutters*) Aye, aye, sir.

EMMA (*slowly and deliberately*) Are you telling me you've no objection to that lad marrying Shirley, *now?*

HENRY. I'd no objections *before*.

EMMA (*gaping*) Now that we know what he is?

HENRY. Now, come on, Emma. Be your age. The poor lad couldn't help being—being born out of wedlock.

EMMA (*unable to believe her ears*) But—do you realize he doesn't even know who his father was?

HENRY (*placidly*) Well—do you?

(EMMA *blinks at him*)

Do you know who *your* father was?

EMMA. *Henry Hornett!*

HENRY. Well, *do* you?

(EMMA, *still darning, rises and moves to* L *of Henry*)

EMMA. You know as well as I do that my father was Ezra Nightingale, and he was married to my mother—Lottie Nightingale.

HENRY (*still placidly; grandly*) Ah, but do you know for *certain* that Ezra Nightingale was your father.

EMMA (*almost bursting with exasperation*) 'Course I do.

HENRY (*maddeningly calmly*) 'Ow? Did your mother ever *tell* you he was?

EMMA. Of course she didn't. (*Rather alarmed*) 'Enry—you never 'eard anything—about my mother, I mean?

HENRY (*placidly*) No, no.

EMMA (*relieved*) Well.

HENRY. Except that she used to go to an awful lot of whist drives——

EMMA (*troubled*) What?

HENRY. —leaving your father at home.

EMMA. Well, 'e didn't like whist drives.

HENRY. But he was asking for trouble—letting her go alone. For all he knows somebody might 'ave trumped her ace.

EMMA. You're not going to tell me you've doubts about *me*, are you?

HENRY (*placidly*) No, Emma. I'm just trying to make you see you're making too much fuss about Albert not being born legal.

EMMA (*moving above the table*) It's not what he's *not*, it's what he *is;* why, everybody's going to call him—a—a . . .

HENRY. Well, what does it matter if they *do?* (*He pauses slightly*) Why, all my pals 'ave been calling me "poor old bastard" for years.

EMMA. Henry Hornett! (*She crosses disgustedly to the sofa and sits on it at the left end*)

HENRY (*rising and moving below the table; still placidly*) Oh, they meant it kindly. They were sympathizing.

EMMA (*angrily*) Oh, if you'd let me get on with what I was saying! How long have you and me been married?

HENRY. Eternity. (*Quickly*) Twenty-three years.

EMMA. Didn't I have to fight like mad to get you?

HENRY. You did.

EMMA. But—I won.

HENRY. Yes, and—(*sotto voce*) I lost.

EMMA. It nearly broke my mother's heart when she saw what I wanted to marry. I had to fight. And here's my own daughter having to fight—to marry the man she wants. D'ye think I've no feelings, Henry? D'ye think I don't feel for Shirley? (*More practically*) She's off her head wanting to marry that lad—nearly as much as I was wanting to marry you.

(HENRY *crosses and sits* R *of Emma on the sofa.*

EDIE, *a changed* EDIE, *bursts in* L. *She is wearing her best dress and a rather odd hat, perhaps it just looks odd on Edie; a long bright scarf of tulle and several other bits of "finery". As she enters she is struggling into a pair of gloves and happily "la-la-ing" the tune of "Love Will Find a Way". She carries her handbag. She twirls gaily as she crosses below the sofa to the mirror* R)

(*She gapes at Edie*) What on earth . . . ?

EDIE. I'm going, I'm going. (*She arranges her scarf and takes a compact from her handbag*)

EMMA (*to Henry; grimly*) This is *it*. This is where we send for the padded ambulance.

EDIE (*gaily*) Oh, I'm not going in a taxi, Emma. (*She covers her face and neck in powder*)

EMMA (*grimly*) We *know* you're not. You've paid National Health for years and if you can't go at their expense, it's a pity. (*She rises, moves above the table and dumps her darning into the work-basket*)

EDIE (*crossing towards the door* L) I must go straight away—before I change my mind.

HENRY (*rising and intercepting Edie below the sofa*) Go where?

EDIE. To the church—for the wedding.

EMMA (*moving to* R *of Edie*) What?

EDIE. Yes, Emma, I've made up my mind. I've crushed my Great Sorrow down inside me and I'm going to see Shirley and Albert married willy-nilly. They are coming together again and I want to be there when they join.

HENRY (*shouting*) But, Edie, I'm telling you . . .

EDIE. I only decided after a great struggle, Henry. Then I put on my best clothes . . .

EMMA (*suddenly*) My best clothes, you mean. (*She points to a clip Edie is wearing*) Where did you get that clip?

EDIE (*faltering*) My—my bottom drawer.

EMMA. My top one! Go and get out of them things.

EDIE. But I can't go to the church without me clothes.

EMMA. Well, you can go and live in a nudist camp if you want, but Lord knows, that'd be the end of the nudists. But get this into your head—there is not going to be a wedding. (*She crosses to the fireplace*)

(HENRY *sits on the chair* L)

EDIE. You mean . . . ? Ooh—(*she moves to* L *of the table and turns on Emma*) you've done it again. And all because poor Albert was born out of wedlock. But I'm warning you, Emma, you're playing fast and loose with fate. Don't do it, Emma. (*She crosses above the sofa to Henry*) Don't let 'er do it, Henry. Shirley and Albert are meant for each other, like Samson and Delilah.

(EDIE *goes into the cupboard under the stairs, sobbing*)

EMMA (*furiously*) Ooh! Edie!

(EDIE *screams, bursts out of the cupboard and exits to the kitchen*)

HENRY (*rising*) Well, at the risk of being hung, drawn and quartered, I'll say there was a grain of sense in what she said. (*He moves sternly to* L *of the table*) Emma, if you stop this marriage . . .

EMMA (*big*) Who *said* I was going to stop it?

HENRY (*blinking at her*) Well, blind O'Reilly! Didn't you say . . . ?

EMMA. I said nothing 'cos I wasn't given the chance; but I'll say it now. If Shirley wants to marry Albert she can—when he's taken his rightful name and *not before*. (*She goes to the sideboard and collects the wedding finery*)

(HENRY *sits on the sofa at the right end*)

There'll be no hocus-pocus, jiggery-pokery with our Shirley. No. Mr Albert Tufnell will have to wait where my daughter's concerned. (*She crosses to the door* L) And that's that. There's going to be no sitting down to dinner before the gong goes.

(EMMA *exits* L)

HENRY (*rising; to himself*) I wish *I'd* never sat down to dinner at all. (*He moves to* R)

(DAPHNE *and* CARNOUSTIE *enter quickly* L. CARNOUSTIE *carries his cap*)

DAPHNE (*moving down* C; *anxiously*) Uncle!

(CARNOUSTIE *moves down* L)

HENRY (*muttering*) Well—what is it now?
DAPHNE. What's the matter with Aunt Emma?
HENRY. Why?
DAPHNE. She's just gone upstairs with a very funny look on her face.
HENRY. She always had a funny look on her face.
DAPHNE. Everything is O.K., isn't it?
HENRY. Daphne, you ought to know your aunt better than that.
CARNOUSTIE. What?
DAPHNE. You mean—it *isn't* O.K.?
HENRY (*muttering*) "Sitting down to dinner before the gong goes."
DAPHNE (*moving to* L *of Henry*) Uncle Henry, what are you talking about? You don't mean she's going to stop Shirley and Albert from getting married?
HENRY. I'm not saying a word.

(DAPHNE *moves up* R *of the table*)

CARNOUSTIE (*crossing to* L *of the table and putting down his cap*) If there should be any hitch noo, what'll Albert do? (*He moves to the window and looks out*)
HENRY. I wouldn't blame him whatever he did. Poor young devil. I'd 'ardly blame 'im if he took his honeymoon first and his wedding after. (*He moves to the kitchen door*) I'm going to my ferrets; with a bit of luck I might get half an hour's peace.
DAPHNE (*looking at Carnoustie and taking Henry's arm*) Yes, well, never mind about your ferrets. (*Wheedling*) Uncle Henry, you do something for me, would you?
HENRY. And what's that?
DAPHNE. Keep Aunt Emma out of our way for a while.
HENRY. I'd like to know how I can do that.
DAPHNE (*leading Henry to the door* L) Well, you can try, anyway.
HENRY (*with a resigned sigh*) Oh, all right. (*He turns to go then stops*) But, dammit, she's in the bedroom. What can I do to keep her in there?
DAPHNE. Surely you can think of *something?*
HENRY (*gaping in horror at her*) I'd like to know *what* you're suggesting.

(HENRY *exits* L. CARNOUSTIE *moves to* R *of the sofa*)

DAPHNE (*moving down* L *of the sofa*) I wonder what's gone wrong now? If Mr Hardcastle said it would be all right for them to . . .
CARNOUSTIE. *He* did—but that old besom's obviously decided otherwise.

DAPHNE. My heart bleeds for those two poor kids. (*She moves to Carnoustie*) One thing I promise you, Scottie, there'll be no nonsense like this over our wedding.

CARNOUSTIE (*rather alarmed*) Our . . . ?

DAPHNE (*smiling*) I did tell you I'd agreed to marry you, didn't I?

CARNOUSTIE. But—ye ha'ena been askit.

DAPHNE (*moving really close to him*) Well, why not "askit" me noo?

CARNOUSTIE (*crossing to the fireplace*) There's a time and place for everything, and this is neither.

(*A door is heard to slam off* L)

Ma Lord, it isn't! (*He quickly hides behind the kitchen door*)

(DAPHNE *runs to the door* L, *opens it and peeps off*)

DAPHNE. It's Albert back. Now for it. (*She closes the door and moves above the table*)

CARNOUSTIE (*emerging and moving to the fireplace*) There'll be battle, murder and sudden death.

DAPHNE. Yes. (*She looks up at the ceiling*) If only the right person could be murdered.

(ALBERT *bursts in* L, *cap in hand.*
SHIRLEY *follows him on, closes the door and stands by it*)

ALBERT (*crossing to Daphne*) Daphne, have you heard the latest? Ma won't let me marry Shirley till I've changed my name.

DAPHNE. But that might take weeks.

ALBERT (*furiously*) 'Course it might, that's what the old So-and-so is counting on. (*He moves to* R *of the sofa*) My leave's up in fourteen days and I've got three months' foreign service to do. (*He sits on the sofa at the left end*)

DAPHNE. But, dammit, Shirley, you're not going to stand for that, are you?

SHIRLEY. What else can I do? If mum says we can't get married then we can't.

DAPHNE. Oh, so you're both just going to sit on your bottoms and do damn-all about it?

SHIRLEY (*crossing below the sofa to Daphne; with spirit*) Now, don't you talk like that, Daphne. When you say "you both" you mean *me*, don't you? I know just what you think of *me*—I'm spineless—tied to mother's apron-strings.

ALBERT. Now look, Shirl—I'm sure Daphne didn't . . .

SHIRLEY (*sweeping on; to Daphne*) But you tell me what *else* we can do. Mum's within her rights forbidding the wedding, and she knows it. (*She sits* R *of Albert on the sofa. On the verge of tears*) It's so easy for you to talk.

DAPHNE (*moving to* R *of the sofa*) Well, all I can say is, Uncle Henry's right.

ALBERT. Uncle Henry?

DAPHNE. He said he wouldn't blame you if you took your honey-moon first and your wedding after.

SHIRLEY. *Dad* said . . . ?

ALBERT (*with a bitter smile*) That's the best idea I've heard today.

DAPHNE (*with sudden intensity*) You've said it, Albert. It *is.*

SHIRLEY (*puzzled*) What?

DAPHNE. That's just what you've got to *do.*

ALBERT (*exasperated*) *What's* just what we've got to do?

DAPHNE. Take your honeymoon first. You were going to Brighton, weren't you?

SHIRLEY. Yes.

DAPHNE (*with emphasis*) Well—go. Take your honeymoon first.

ALBERT (*stunned*) Blimey!

CARNOUSTIE (*horrified*) Of all the immoral and revoltin' ideas . . .

DAPHNE (*firmly*) Quiet, you. It'll be your turn to holler in a minute.

CARNOUSTIE (*more firmly*) I'll holler now. I've never hearrd such downright wickedness.

DAPHNE (*moving towards Carnoustie*) Scottie, *please.*

CARNOUSTIE. And if you think Albert would be party to such a plan . . .

DAPHNE (*moving to* L *of Carnoustie; firmly but not hastily*) Will you for the love of Annie Laurie and Bonnie Mary of Argyll, please— (*she raises her voice a little*) shut up!

(CARNOUSTIE'S *mouth closes abruptly*)

Thank you. (*She crosses to* C) Now . . .

ALBERT. But, Daphne . . .

DAPHNE. Albert, it's your only hope.

SHIRLEY. Go to Brighton—as if we were married? Do you think I'd do a thing like that?

DAPHNE. I'd like Aunt Emma to *think* you'd done it. Don't you see? If she thought you *had,* she'd run you and Albert to the church so fast you'd be married before you realized it.

ALBERT (*to Shirley*) She's right, honey. But, Daphne, if Shirley and me go off alone . . .

DAPHNE. Oh, no, no. You won't be alone. *We'll* be with you.

ALBERT. "We"?

DAPHNE (*pointing to herself*) Me and—(*she points to Carnoustie*) him.

CARNOUSTIE (*with a yelp*) What?

DAPHNE (*crossing smilingly to Carnoustie*) I told you it would soon be your turn to start hollering. Well, go on—holler.

CARNOUSTIE (*wildly*) Is there no limit to your sinfulness, wumman? Not only do you suggest that Albert and Shirley—misbehave them-selves, but now you're trying to entice me into . . . (*Fervently*) May the Lord forgi'e ye!

DAPHNE (*smiling*) Well, we'd better start working on you first, to clean up that nasty mind of yours.

CARNOUSTIE. Eh?

DAPHNE. What I'm suggesting is that we go with Shirley and Albert—playing gooseberry. Aunt Emma won't know it, but Shirley and I will be sharing one room and you and Albert the other.

CARNOUSTIE (*blinking*) Och!

DAPHNE (*smiling*) And take that look of disappointment off your face—it's indecent.

ALBERT (*rising excitedly*) You know, you've got something there, Daphne. What do you say, Shirl? It's up to you. Dare we?

SHIRLEY (*rising; in a whisper, but firmly*) Yes, Albert—yes. (*She hugs him*)

ALBERT. That's my girl.

DAPHNE. Good for you. Now—(*she moves above the table*) you're all packed up, aren't you, Albert?

ALBERT. You bet I am.

DAPHNE. And you are, Scottie?

CARNOUSTIE (*still wildly*) I've no' said I agreed. I've got to gie the matter an awfu' lot o' thocht.

DAPHNE. You can give it all the thought you like—when you're in the train.

SHIRLEY (*crossing to L of Daphne*) We can catch the three o'clock just as we planned. I'll slip upstairs quietly and get ready. We'll want a taxi.

ALBERT (*moving towards the door L*) I'll get one.

SHIRLEY. He'd better not come up to the house, though—tell him to wait at the end of the street and we'll slip out the back way. (*Excitedly*) Oh, dear! Is there anything else?

CARNOUSTIE (*moving to R of the table; firmly*) Aye, there is. How d'y' know we'll get another room at the hotel?

ALBERT. I'll phone 'em while I'm out.

CARNOUSTIE. Ye'll make it clear about the bookings, mind. We don't want any misunderstandings when we get down there. None o' that "Mr and Mrs" nonsense.

SHIRLEY (*suddenly*) Albert! Our bags.

ALBERT. What about them?

SHIRLEY. They're still labelled "Mr and Mrs".

CARNOUSTIE (*almost hooting*) Then take 'em off. I'll no' stand for it.

DAPHNE. You're right, sweetheart, you won't. (*She pushes Carnoustie on to the chair R of the table*) You'll just sit down and write out some new labels. Have you got some, Shirley?

SHIRLEY (*crossing to the sideboard*) Yes. I think there are some in here. (*She takes some labels from the sideboard drawer*)

CARNOUSTIE. What's the name of this hotel?

(ALBERT *takes out a letter and hands it to Carnoustie*)

ALBERT. It's on this letter here. (*He moves below the sofa*)

SHIRLEY (*putting the labels on the table*) There's the labels.

(CARNOUSTIE *addresses the labels*. DAPHNE *looks over his shoulder*)

Albert . . . (*She crosses to Albert*)

ALBERT. Just going. (*He suddenly sweeps Shirley into his arms, kisses her, then smiles at her*) Trust me to behave myself at Brighton?

CARNOUSTIE. She can trust me to see you do.

ALBERT (*collecting his cap*) Be ready in five minutes. O.K.?

DAPHNE. Off you go, Shirley, I'll be with you in a minute.

(SHIRLEY *crosses to the door* L, *as* ALBERT *crosses to the door* R. *They both turn, smile and throw a kiss to each other.*
ALBERT *exits to the kitchen.*
SHIRLEY *exits* L)

(*She moves to the mirror* R) It *is* a bit of an anxious moment, isn't it?

CARNOUSTIE. I'm glad ye show some appreciation o' the terrible risks ye're taking. Bringing two unmarried people together at the very time and in the very place where they w'uld have been spending the best part o' their honeymoon.

DAPHNE (*shaking her head and moving to* R *of Carnoustie*) But—they're not sharing a bedroom.

CARNOUSTIE. Wumman! Hold your whisst. (*He rises and moves below the table*)

DAPHNE. Shirley's in no more danger from Albert than I am from you. And the Lord knows, that's not much.

CARNOUSTIE. I wu' no' be too sure.

DAPHNE. About them, or—(*hopefully*) us?

CARNOUSTIE. I'm talking aboot men and wummen—in general. (*Ponderously*) Aboot the awful fiery element in their natures, which is stronger than their sense of decency.

DAPHNE (*moving to* R *of him*) Carn-nous-tie!

CARNOUSTIE. Wull?

DAPHNE. Have *you* got a fiery element!

CARNOUSTIE (*moving down* L *of the sofa*) You're mocking me, now. You think I'm not capable of great emotion. But I'll ha' ye know that at times I'm carried awa' on a mighty tide of passion.

DAPHNE (*moving to him*) Carnoustie, is it high tide now?

CARNOUSTIE. Aye, it is. (*He suddenly seizes Daphne in his arms and kisses her*)

(MRS LACK *enters from the kitchen and closes the door*)

MRS LACK. Oh, pardon me, I'm sure.

(CARNOUSTIE *leaps away down* L. DAPHNE *moves above the sofa*)

CARNOUSTIE. Mrs Lack—I . . .

MRS LACK. Oh, there's no need to apologize. I was young myself once.

DAPHNE (*crossing to the door* L) If you'll excuse me, I . . .

MRS LACK (*making a big thing of turning away to examine the box of presents*) Don't mind me.

DAPHNE (*to Carnoustie; under her breath*) Get rid of her. (*To Mrs Lack*) I'll just pop up and see Shirley.

(DAPHNE *exits* L)

MRS LACK (*moving to* R *of the table*) Sorry to be a spoil-sport, but I wanted to see Mrs Hornett.

CARNOUSTIE. She's upstairs in her room, I think. (*He takes a magazine from the trolley, perches on the left arm of the sofa and pretends to read*)

MRS LACK. Well, what's the latest? Are those two getting married, or aren't they?

CARNOUSTIE. I'm no' at liberty to discuss Albert's and Shirley's affairs.

MRS LACK. Hoity-toity!

CARNOUSTIE. And, if you'll forgive me saying it, it's no' business o' yours.

MRS LACK. I am a friend of the family, I hope. (*She glances at a label on the table, then seeing Carnoustie's back is turned towards her, she quickly picks up the label, looks at it then replaces it on the table*) And if I'm not allowed to show a bit of interest in . . .

(CARNOUSTIE *rises, throws down the magazine, crosses to the table, picks up the labels and the letter, puts them in his blouse then crosses down* R)

CARNOUSTIE. It seems to me there's an awful lot of people roond here taking too much interest in things that don't concern 'em, if you ask me.

MRS LACK (*not really listening to him; excitedly*) Excuse me—(*she crosses to the door* L) I've got to see Emma. She is upstairs, you say.

(MRS LACK *exits quickly* L)

CARNOUSTIE. There are different ways of taking interest, you know . . . (*He realizes Mrs Lack has gone*) She's no' interested. (*He moves to the cases, puts them on the sofa, at the left end, takes out the labels and sorts them*)

(EDIE *enters from the kitchen, carrying an evening paper.* CARNOUSTIE *has his back to her and does not hear her come in.* EDIE *looks around as if expecting disaster and suddenly sees Carnoustie*)

EDIE (*with a little squeak*) Oh. (*She closes the door*)

CARNOUSTIE (*turning with a little yelp*) Oh. (*He puts the labels in his blouse. Nervously*) It's you, Aunt Edie.

EDIE (*putting the paper on the sideboard and moving to* R *of the table*) Has Emma been asking for me?

CARNOUSTIE. No, no.

EDIE (*almost in a whisper*) Where is everybody?

CARNOUSTIE. Och—roond and aboot. (*Vaguely*) Roond and aboot.

EDIE (*crossing to Carnoustie*) What's happening, Carnoustie? Are Shirley and Albert getting married? Nobody tells me nothing.

CARNOUSTIE (*nervously*) Dinna' worry your bonnie wee heid, Aunt Edie. Everything'll work oot fine—just you see. (*He moves to the window and looks out*)

EDIE (*her voice quivering*) Oh, I *do* hope so. I do want Shirley to be happy.

(CARNOUSTIE *moves to* R *of Edie*)

It isn't fair that *she* should go through life with a Great Sorrow. (*Almost in tears*) Mind you, I wouldn't be without mine for the world. It gives me something to live with. But Shirley—no. (*The tears begin to flow*)

CARNOUSTIE (*very embarrassed*) Aunt Edie . . .

(EDIE'S *tears flow faster, to the accompaniment of sobbing*)

(*He sits Edie on the sofa and crouches beside her*) There, there, dinna greet, Aunt Edie. Come on, now. (*He puts his hand under her chin and raises her face*) Let me see you smile. Come on, now, give me a big smile.

(EDIE *stops sobbing for a moment, looks into Carnoustie's eyes, then suddenly breaks down again and positively howls*)

EDIE. Oh, I can't, Carnoustie. (*She clasps him round the neck*)

CARNOUSTIE (*muttering*) Ma Lord!

(ALBERT *dashes in from the kitchen*)

ALBERT (*above the table*) It's all fixed . . . (*He breaks off*)

(CARNOUSTIE *rises with* EDIE *still clinging round his neck, her feet well clear of the floor*)

What . . . ?

(CARNOUSTIE *staggers desperately to* ALBERT *who manages to take* EDIE *from him, holding her like a child*)

CARNOUSTIE. Albert, it's Aunt Edie.

ALBERT (*exasperated*) So I see.

CARNOUSTIE. She's greetin'.

ALBERT. So I hear. What are we going to do? It's time we were off.

(EDIE *suddenly jumps from Albert's arms and stands* R *of him*)

EDIE. Off? You're not going, Albert love?

ALBERT. Yes, Aunt Edie. Now, you were enjoying your cry, weren't you?

EDIE (*vigorously nodding her head*) Yes. But . . .

ALBERT. Then why don't you—(*he looks desperately around*) just go quietly into a corner and finish it out? (*He leads Edie to the fireplace*)

(CARNOUSTIE *goes to the door* L, *opens it a little and peers off*)

Now, you stand there, Aunt Edie—(*he turns her to face the fireplace*) with your back to us. Cover your eyes, and don't turn round. You see, something's going to happen that . . .

EDIE (*turning*) Happen? What?

ALBERT. Something it's best you know nothing about. (*He turns her to face* R) And what you don't see you can't talk about, can you?

CARNOUSTIE. Albert! The girls are here.

ALBERT. Let's get their bags. (*He dashes to the sofa and collects his bag*)

> (CARNOUSTIE *opens the door wide.*
> SHIRLEY *enters* L, *carrying a suitcase.*
> DAPHNE *follows her on, carrying a suitcase. The girls are in outdoor clothes.* EDIE *turns with a squeak and seeing the cases, dithers with fright*)

EDIE. "Bags"? Albert!

> (DAPHNE *gives her case to* CARNOUSTIE, *who closes the door and collects his case from the sofa*)

ALBERT (*desperately*) Aunt Edie, I told you not to turn round.

EDIE. Eloping! (*Near hysteria, she moves to* R *of the table*) You can't do it, Shirley. Albert, love, you can't *do* it. It's flying in the face of—Emma.

DAPHNE. So long as we're *flying*, Aunt Edie, what the hell?

EDIE. Daphne! You're not going—with Carnoustie?

DAPHNE. Uh-huh!

EDIE (*wailing*) But you can't. You're not even *engaged*. And he's a sailor, and Emma knows what sailors are. (*She rushes to block the kitchen door*)

ALBERT (*crossing to the kitchen door*) Out of the way, Aunt Edie.

EDIE (*spreading her arms wide*) I've got to stop you. My conscience tells me, I've got to stop you. (*Suddenly and loudly*) Stop!

SHIRLEY. Aunt *Edie!*

EDIE (*loudly*) Stop! (*But as she shouts, she opens the kitchen door and frantically waves her arms indicating "Go"*) Stop! (*She waves*)

ALBERT (*grinning*) Bless you, Aunt Edie.

> (ALBERT, SHIRLEY and DAPHNE *exit to the kitchen, then can be seen passing the window.* CARNOUSTIE *moves to the kitchen door*)

EDIE. Stop!

> (CARNOUSTIE *stops*)

(*Irritably*) What are you stopping for?

> (CARNOUSTIE *exits to the kitchen, then can be seen passing the window*)

F

(*She calls hysterically out of the window*) Write to me from Gretna Green. (*She flings up her arms and, overbalancing, falls into the box of presents. With a great struggle, she emerges unhurt and throws herself on to the sofa*) It's wonderful—it's wonderful. It's the end of the world.

> (*There is a loud and agonized cry from* SHIRLEY, *off, and a confused babel of angry and distressed voices.*
> SHIRLEY *and* DAPHNE *are seen returning past the window*)

(*She stiffens suddenly with horror*) What—what's happening?

> (SHIRLEY *rushes in from the kitchen in a flood of noisy tears and collapses into the easy chair.* EDIE *jumps up, runs up to Shirley and crouches beside her*)

Oh—no! Shirley, my poor lamb, what . . . ?

> (DAPHNE *storms in from the kitchen*)

DAPHNE (*as she enters*) Shirley, if you let her get away with it *this* time you can take it from me that you'll be saying good-bye to Albert for good and all.

EDIE (*almost demented*) Daphne, Daphne! What's happened? Why doesn't anybody ever tell me anything? Daphne . . .

DAPHNE (*snapping*) Keep away from me, Aunt Edie!

EDIE. What?

DAPHNE. At this moment I'm not responsible for my actions. You come near me and I'm liable to crown you.

EDIE. Daphne! (*She sits on the pouffe, facing up stage*)

> (DAPHNE *stands by the fireplace.*
> ALBERT *and* CARNOUSTIE *are seen backing outside the window, closely followed by* HENRY, EMMA *and* MRS LACK. HENRY *carries a long-handled rake.* EMMA *brandishes a broom and* MRS LACK *has a mop.*
> ALBERT *enters from the kitchen, carrying his own and Shirley's cases. He stands up* C *and puts the cases on the floor by the window.*
> CARNOUSTIE *enters from the kitchen, carrying his own and Daphne's cases. He stands above the easy chair and puts the cases on the floor.*
> HENRY *enters from the kitchen and stands* L *of Carnoustie.*
> EMMA *follows him on and stands above the table.*
> MRS LACK *enters from the kitchen and stands up* L *of Emma. They are all talking at once*)

ALBERT. I'm warning you, Pop, if you do so much as touch me with that ruddy thing, I'll smash this place up into matchwood, even if I get five years for doing it.

CARNOUSTIE. I've never been so insulted in ma life. I'm no' a child, I'd have you know. I'm a man. And a man's a man for a' that—an' a' that.

> (*As* EMMA *enters, all the speeches except* HENRY'S *come to an end*)

HENRY. Now, look here, Albert, we've got to talk this thing over.

EMMA (*raging*) I'll say we're going to talk things over. (*Sharply*) Florrie.

MRS LACK (*eagerly*) Yes, Emma?

EMMA (*pointing to the door* L) Stand over by that door and if either of these two—(*she indicates Albert and Carnoustie*) try to bolt through it, you have my permission to strike 'em unconscious.

(MRS LACK *goes to the door* L *and stands in front of it with her mop* "*at the ready*")

(*Sharper still*) Henry! Close that door. Stand in front of it, and if you let this couple through it I promise you I'll strike you unconscious.

(HENRY *closes the door.* EMMA *thrusts her broom at* HENRY, *who takes it and leans it in the corner up* R)

EDIE (*rising; tremulously*) Emma—you mustn't . . .

EMMA (*turning on Edie*) Oh, you're unconscious, anyway.

(EDIE *sits on the pouffe*)

(*She turns on Albert*) Well, Mr Albert—what-ever-your-name-is. You'd got it all nicely planned, hadn't you? "If we can't have a wedding," you said, "we'll do without it. What does it matter so long as the results are the same."

ALBERT (*moving to* R *of the sofa*) Of all the . . .

CARNOUSTIE (*moving to* L *of the easy chair*) If I don't get oot of this house soon, I'll . . .

EMMA (*turning on Carnoustie*) Yes, and *you* weren't going to be left out in the cold, were you?

CARNOUSTIE (*yelping*) What!

EMMA (*sweeping on*) "Let's make it a gathering of the clans. Let's make it an orgy. What about it, Daphne?" (*With a glare at Daphne*) And I'll bet he didn't have to ask you twice.

DAPHNE. I'm getting out of this house.

EMMA. You'll get out quick enough when I say so and not before —and it *won't* be to Brighton with Harry Lauder here. (*She turns to Shirley*) And as for you, my girl . . .

SHIRLEY (*almost screaming*) Mum, if you'd only be quiet for a minute and listen to reason . . .

ALBERT. "Listen"! (*He moves to* L *of the table*) She's never even heard of the word, have you, Ma? You'd have to look it up in a dictionary to find out what it means.

EMMA (*to Shirley*) Were you going to Brighton with this lot or weren't you?

SHIRLEY. Yes, I was, Mum, but . . .

EMMA (*to Henry*) See! Out of the mouth of babes and ducklings . . .

ALBERT (*moving to* R *of the sofa*) But you don't know why we were going!

EMMA (*moving to* R *of the table*) Don't I? I may not have been in the Navy, my lad, but I know the facts of life as well as you. (*Suddenly*) Don't I, Henry?

HENRY (*moving above the table; mumbling*) Yes, you certainly taught me a trick or two.

EMMA (*shutting him up*) Thank you, Henry—you've said your piece. (*To the others*) There's only one reason why unmarried couples go to Brighton, and it is not to eat jellied eels.

DAPHNE. We were going to Brighton 'cos I suggested it. We were all going to the same hotel. But separate rooms. Shirley and me in one room and Albert and Carnoustie in the other.

EMMA. You expect me to believe that?

DAPHNE. No, Aunt Emma, I don't, because you haven't got the sort of mind that *could* believe it. But I'll tell you this. I wouldn't have blamed Albert and Shirley if they'd done what Uncle Henry suggested.

(HENRY *makes frantic signals behind Emma's back to Daphne*)

—taken their honeymoon first and their wedding after. (*She realizes what she has said. Horrified*) Oh!

(HENRY *makes a strategic retreat towards the kitchen*)

EMMA (*turning slowly to Henry*) Henry! Come back!

(HENRY *moves above the table*)

(*Ominously*) You'll deny that, Henry.

HENRY. It—it was only a joke.

EMMA. It was downright wickedness. From first to last you've been the cause of all the trouble.

ALBERT. You'd better listen to me, Mrs Hornett. None of us had anything in mind that was the least wrong. But that doesn't matter now. What matters is this. You're determined I shan't marry Shirley.

SHIRLEY (*rising*) But I'm going to marry him, Mother, whether you want me to or not. (*She crosses to Albert*) You've got to believe that, Albert. Nothing mother can say will make me change my mind. And if you want proof of that I'm ready to go to Brighton with you now—on any terms.

(ALBERT *puts his arms around Shirley*)

EMMA. You'll go on my terms only, my girl. I'll have none of this hire-purchase business—no deposit, take the goods away and pay when you feel inclined. (*She takes a long deep breath*) Oh, no! (*To Albert*) Not a foot will you stir out of this house with my daughter till you're properly married.

ALBERT (*frenzied*) Isn't that what I *want* to do—marry Shirl? Isn't that what I've wanted all along?

EMMA. And have I ever said you can't?

ALBERT (*flabbergasted*) Blind O'Reilly! (*He breaks from Shirley and sits on the sofa at the left end*)

(SHIRLEY *sits* R *of Albert on the sofa.* MRS LACK *moves down* L)

EMMA. I may have had a moment of doubt when I read that tele-gram—but once I knew the facts I accepted the inedible. I resigned myself to "what will be, must be"—"*che seri, sara*".

HENRY. And *I* resigned myself to listening to you saying so.

(*The front-door bell rings*)

EMMA (*shouting towards the kitchen*) Edie!

EDIE (*rising and rushing to* R *of Emma*) Yes, Emma?

EMMA (*startled*) Oh. Well, go on, answer it.

(EDIE *crosses to the door* L)

And whoever it is and whatever they want, tell 'em "no".

EDIE. No.

(EDIE *exits* R, *closing the door behind her*)

EMMA. Well, Florrie, I'm sure I'm very grateful to you for letting me know what this little lot were up to.

(DAPHNE *perches on the right arm of the easy chair*)

MRS LACK (*moving below the sofa; happily*) I only did my duty, Emma.

EMMA (*with a sniff*) *You* might call it that. But some might call it poking your nose into other people's business—as usual.

MRS LACK (*bridling*) What!

EMMA (*sweeping on*) However—it was all for the best, this time, so I'll overlook it.

(MRS LACK *retires* L.
    EDIE *rushes in* L *to* L *of the table*)

EDIE (*excitedly*) Emma! It's him! He's come back!

EMMA. Who? And didn't you tell him "No"?

(HARDCASTLE *enters* L *and stands down* L *of the sofa*)

HARDCASTLE (*as he enters*) Forgive me for barging in once more, but . . .

(SHIRLEY *rises*)

ALBERT ⎫   ⎧ (*He leaps to attention*) Sir!
CARNOUSTIE ⎬ (*together*) ⎨ (*He leaps to attention and salutes*) Sirrr!
HENRY ⎭   ⎩ (*He salutes*) Sir!

EMMA. Relax, Hornett.

(HENRY *relaxes*)

(*To Carnoustie*) And you.

(CARNOUSTIE *relaxes*)

(*To Albert*) And you.

(ALBERT *relaxes and moves to* L *of the sofa*)

(*To Hardcastle*) There, I've said it *for* you. And *now* what?
HARDCASTLE. I had to come back. (*He crosses to* L *of the table*)

(EDIE *gives Hardcastle a deep curtsy then retires, confused, and stands* R *of the sofa*)

(*He tries to ignore Edie*) Thimble, when I called a little while ago, I'm afraid I dropped a clanger.
EMMA. Well, pick it up and take it away and good afternoon.

(EDIE *goes on her knees in front of Hardcastle*)

Edie, what are you doing?
EDIE. I'm looking for his clanger. (*She rises and moves above the sofa*)

(HARDCASTLE *throws his cap on to the table in exasperation*)

HARDCASTLE (*turning to Albert*) I think I told you that if you wanted to change your name it would take a very considerable time. But when I phoned the Captain just now, he told me that was quite incorrect. In English law, apparently, any man can change his name simply by making a declaration over a sixpenny stamp and having it witnessed. A solicitor would do the job in five minutes.

ALBERT ⎫
SHIRLEY ⎬ (*together*)
DAPHNE ⎭

{ (*Excitedly*) You mean that, sir? (*He moves to* L *of Shirley*)
(*To Albert*) Five minutes. Ooh! Y'hear that, Albert?
Well! What do you know?

(HENRY, MRS LACK *and* EDIE *make noises of approval*)

EMMA (*sitting* R *of the table; firmly*) I don't believe it.
HARDCASTLE. What!
EMMA. I say, I don't believe it.
ALL (*ad lib.*) Oh, you can't . . . You're not going to . . . (*Etc., etc.*)
EMMA (*firmer than ever*) I don't believe it.

(*There is a deadly silence*)

(*She rises*) It's too good to be true. (*She beams on everybody*)

(*There are whoops of delight from the others*)

SHIRLEY. Mum, you mean that?
EMMA (*sharply*) 'Course I mean it. I'm your mother, aren't I? (*With a glare at Henry*) That's more than your father can say. (*To Shirley*) All I've wanted—all I've fought tooth and nail for is to see that when you married you married happy. But I've never tried to stop you—never. (*She glares around*) Who says I have?

(*There is silence*)

(*To Hardcastle. Briskly*) But now, young man—if you've got your facts right, for once, and a sixpenny stamp will do the trick . . .

HARDCASTLE. I assure you, Mrs Hornett . . .

EMMA (*moving down* L *of the table and rapping out orders*) Right! Edie!
Up to the post office and get a sixpenny stamp.

(EDIE *rushes out* L)

Henry! Go and ring up a solicitor and tell him we're all coming to
see him—with a sixpenny stamp. Newcastle—go and get a taxi.

HARDCASTLE. Yes. (*He moves* L *then realizes and stops*) What?

EMMA. Shirley! (*She suddenly softens*) Shirley—come and give your
old mother a kiss.

SHIRLEY (*rushing into Emma's arms*) Mum! Oh, Mum!

EMMA (*sobbing loudly*) I know, I know.

SHIRLEY. Oh, Mum!

ALBERT (*gaping at Emma*) I'd never have believed it possible.

(SHIRLEY *tears herself from Emma's embraces and rushes to Albert*)

SHIRLEY. Albert! (*She embraces him*)

(EMMA *wipes her eyes with a large handkerchief*)

HARDCASTLE (*stepping forward*) Mrs Hornett . . .

EMMA (*putting out her hand to ward off Hardcastle*) Now then, none
of that.

Quick CURTAIN

FURNITURE AND PROPERTY LIST

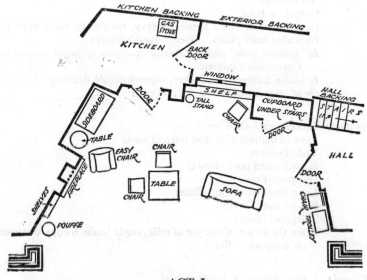

ACT I

On stage: Table. *On it:* chenille cloth, bouquet, posy, veil
4 upright chairs
Sofa. *On it:* cushions, antimacassar
Easy chair. *On it:* cushion, antimacassar, Henry's jacket with
     buttonhole, tie and stiff collar
    Under it: Emma's shoes
Pouffe
Sideboard. *On it:* runner, Albert's and Carnoustie's caps, clothes
    brush, darning basket with socks, wool, etc., plate
    In drawer: white handkerchief, Biro, writing pad,
    luggage labels
Shelves (down R) *On them:* books, magazines, table-lamp
Tall stand. *On it:* bowl of flowers
Trolley (L) *On it:* ashtray, portable radio, magazines, vase of
 flowers, books in bookends
Small table (above fireplace) *On it:* radio
Over mantelpiece: mirror, portrait of the Queen
On mantelpiece: clock, ornaments, bottle of aspirin, ashtray,
 tobacco pouch, pipe, matches, other suitable dressing

In grate: paper fan
Fender
Coal seuttle
Fire-irons
Hearth rug
Heavy window curtains
Net curtains
Carpet on floor
On window-sill: china figure, ashtray, tea caddy, large brass pot
On walls: wall plates, velvet-framed pictures
In cupboard under stairs: Albert's suitcase, raincoat and scarf,
    Carnoustie's suitcase
In kitchen backing: gas cooker, other suitable dressing
On off stage side of kitchen door: overall

Off stage: Saucer, teacloth (EDIE)
    Piece of blanket with iron burn (EMMA)
    Veil (DAPHNE)
    Bouquet and posy (EMMA)
    Dustpan (EDIE)
    Long-handled broom (EDIE)
    Bowler hat (HENRY)
    Telegram (EDIE)
    Tray. *On it:* pot of tea, jug of milk, sugar basin, 6 cups, 6 saucers,
        6 teaspoons (EDIE)

Personal: EMMA: handbag, handkerchief
    CARNOUSTIE: cigarettes, wedding ring
    ALBERT: lighter, handkerchief
    SHIRLEY: handkerchief
    EDIE: handkerchief
    MRS LACK: handbag. *In it:* compact, lipstick, pencil, diary
    HENRY: *in turn-ups*—dust, matchsticks, cigarette end

ACT II

Setting as at the end of Act I

Off stage: Basket (EDIE)
    Tray. *On it:* 2 cups of tea (MRS LACK)
    Brief-case. *In it:* documents and folders (HARDCASTLE)

Personal: HENRY: pools coupon, pencil, piece of paper
    MRS LACK: key

ACT III

Setting as at the end of Act **II**

Off stage: Large cardboard box. *In it:* wedding presents, lampshade, orna-
            ments in two pieces (EDIE)
            Basket. *In it:* sandwiches wrapped in greaseproof paper (EDIE)
            Evening paper (EDIE)
            Suitcase (SHIRLEY)
            Suitcase (DAPHNE)
            Long-handled rake (HENRY)
            Broom (EMMA)
            Mop (MRS LACK)

Personal: HARDCASTLE: watch
            EDIE: clip, handbag. *In it:* compact
            ALBERT: hotel letter
            EMMA: large handkerchief

LIGHTING PLOT

Property fittings required: none

    Interior. A living-room. The same scene throughout

    THE APPARENT SOURCE OF LIGHT is a window back c

    THE MAIN ACTING AREAS are up c, at a sofa lc, at an easy chair r and
    at a table c

ACT I.   Late morning

To open: Effect of morning sunshine

No cues

ACT II.   Lights as at the end of the previous Act

No cues

ACT III.   Lights as at the end of the previous Act

No cues

EFFECTS PLOT

ACT I

Cue 1   ALBERT: "I wonder."   (Page 4)
Sound of women's voices outside window

Cue 2   ALBERT closes window   (Page 4)
Voices cease

Cue 3   EDIE opens the window   (Page 7)
Sound of women's voices

Cue 4   ALBERT closes window   (Page 7)
Voices cease

Cue 5   EDIE: ". . . into the kitchen."   (Page 8)
Door slam

Cue 6   DAPHNE: ". . . Uncle Henry, I'll . . ."   (Page 10)
Minor crash in kitchen

Cue 7   EMMA opens the window   (Page 16)
Sound of women's voices for a short time

Cue 8   EMMA: ". . . us a chance."   (Page 17)
Sound of taxi horn

Cue 9   EMMA: ". . . an empty syphon."   (Page 23)
Front-door bell rings

Cue 10   EMMA: ". . . wishes she'll need."   (Page 24)
Front-door bell rings

Cue 11   EMMA: ". . . all ready, 'cos . . ."   (Page 24)
Sound of taxi horn

Cue 12   EMMA: "The telegram."   (Page 24)
Front-door bell rings

ACT II

Cue 13   EMMA: "We don't want you . . ."   (Page 36)
Terrific door slam off L.

Cue 14   CARNOUSTIE: "Aye!"   (Page 51)
Door slam off L.

ACT III

Cue 15 HARDCASTLE: ". . . a spinster."   (Page 59)
          Front-door bell rings

Cue 16 ALBERT: ". . . I suppose."   (Page 59)
          Front-door bell rings

Cue 17 EDIE: "I can't hear . . ."   (Page 59)
          Front door-bell rings

Cue 18 CARNOUSTIE: ". . . this is neither."   (Page 71)
          Door slam off L

Cue 19 HENRY: ". . . you saying so "   (Page 81)
          Front-door bell rings

7652 34 89